WOMEN PATH-BREAKERS

Stories of Success and Strength

CONTENTS

Research and Script: Tripti Nainwal
Colourists: Ramesh C., Silambarasan K. and Sanjhiya Mayekar
Special Pages Illustrations: Ketan Pal
Layout: Ketan Pal
Cover Art: Animesh Debnath
Art Director: Savio Mascarenhas
Deputy Editor: Sanjana Kapur

Executive Editor: Reena Ittyerah Puri

Pandita Ramabai - Changing the lives of child brides and widows

*PRIME MINISTER OF THE MARATHA EMPIRE
^A SHLOKA IN PRAISE OF GANESHA
**NOW KNOWN AS PUNE

WHEN ANANT EXCITEDLY TOLD HIS WIFE -
WHAT ARE YOU SAYING? THE GODS WILL FROWN ON US IF I DO THAT!
SHE'S RIGHT. DO YOU WANT TO BRING RUIN TO OUR FAMILY?
BUT.. BUT....
ANANT WAS HELPLESS IN THE FACE OF THEIR BELIEF AND FEAR. HE HAD TO LET IT GO BUT HE NEVER FORGOT.

MANY YEARS LATER, HIS WIFE DIED. AS WAS THE CUSTOM, ANOTHER MARRIAGE WAS PROPOSED FOR HIM, THIS TIME TO NINE-YEAR-OLD LAKSHMIBAI. BUT BEFORE THE MARRIAGE COULD BE FIXED -
I AGREE TO THIS MARRIAGE, ONLY IF YOU ALLOW ME TO EDUCATE HER.
THAT'S A STRANGE REQUEST! MOST PEOPLE WANT MONEY.
ANANT WAS 44 YEARS OLD.
THIS TIME, ANANT'S OWN FAMILY DID NOT OBJECT EITHER BUT THE NEIGHBOURS WERE SHOCKED.
HE'LL RUIN OUR NEIGHBOURHOOD!
HE'S BRINGING SHAME TO OUR CASTE!

REALISING THAT HE WOULD NEVER BE ALLOWED TO LIVE IN PEACE, ANANT TOOK HIS WIFE AND MOVED INTO THE JUNGLE OF GANGAMULA, NEAR MANGALORE. THE FIRST NIGHT WAS TERRIFYING.
GROWL
GRRR GRRRR
AHHHHHH!
GO TO SLEEP. THE FIRE WILL KEEP THE TIGER AWAY.

GRADUALLY, THEY SETTLED DOWN ON THE OUTSKIRTS OF THE FOREST. YOUNG LEARNERS BEGAN COMING TO ANANT SHASTRI FOR HIS KNOWLEDGE. LAKSHMIBAI TOO EXCELLED IN SANSKRIT.

OVER THE YEARS, SIX CHILDREN WERE BORN TO THE COUPLE OUT OF WHICH ONLY THREE SURVIVED. THE YOUNGEST WAS RAMA, A LOVELY BABY GIRL BORN ON 23 APRIL, 1858.
LOOK AT RAMA! SHE IS WALKING BY HERSELF!
THOUGH MONEY WAS SCARCE, THE CHILDREN GREW UP FAR AND FREE FROM SOCIETY. THE PARENTS SHOWERED THEM WITH LOVE.

BUT BY THE TIME RAMA WAS NINE, THE FAMILY BECAME VERY POOR. SO, THEY STARTED GOING ON LONG JOURNEYS TO HOLY SHRINES. ANANT SHASTRI WOULD READ VERSES FROM THE PURANAS TO PILGRIMS IN EXCHANGE FOR SOME MONEY.
HE ALSO USED THIS OPPORTUNITY TO TALK ABOUT EDUCATING GIRLS. THE PRIESTS DISAPPROVED OF THIS. AS A RESULT, HE DID NOT EARN MUCH.

DURING THEIR TRAVELS, LAKSHMIBAI TAUGHT RAMA AND HER SIBLINGS. BY THE TIME RAMA WAS 13, SHE HAD LEARNT MANY LANGUAGES AND WAS WELL-VERSED IN SANSKRIT. SHE WAS ALSO OBSERVANT AND INTELLIGENT.
WHATEVER MONEY FATHER MAKES, HE GIVES TO THE PRIESTS BELIEVING THAT THE GODS WILL BLESS US.
THAT'S OUR FAITH, RAMA. THE GODS MUST BE SATISFIED.

RAMA COULD ALSO SEE THE VARIOUS WAYS BY WHICH INNOCENT PILGRIMS WERE BEING CHEATED.

BUT NOTHING REALLY HAPPENS EVEN AFTER GIVING SO MUCH MONEY. ARE OUR GODS REALLY UNKIND?

OF COURSE NOT! WAIT AND SEE.

AS THE YEARS PASSED BY –

THERE IS NO MONEY LEFT. NO FOOD. THE CHILDREN ARE FALLING ILL ALL THE TIME.

IT WAS 1874, THE YEAR WHEN A GREAT FAMINE SWEPT THE COUNTRY. FOOD WAS SCARCE AND THE DONGRE FAMILY HAD NONE.

IN A SWEEP OF MISFORTUNE, FIRST ANANT SHASTRI DIED OF STARVATION, THEN LAKSHMIBAI AND AFTER THAT, THE ELDEST DAUGHTER. THREE MEMBERS OF THE FAMILY HAD DIED WITHIN A FEW MONTHS!

NOW THERE WERE JUST TWO LEFT, RAMA AND HER ELDER BROTHER, SRINIVASA.

WHERE WILL WE GO? WHAT WILL WE DO?

RAMA WAS ONLY 16 AND SRINIVASA, 18. THEY HAD NO FAMIL
LEFT AND NO POSSESSIONS TO BANK UPON. THE ONLY THIN
THEY KNEW WAS WHAT THEIR PARENTS HAD TAUGHT THEM.

*MODERN-DAY KOLKATA
^GODDESS OF WISDOM

AT LAST IT SEEMS LIKE WE CAN REST!
YES, WE FINALLY HAVE A HOME.

SOON, BOTH SIBLINGS BECAME RESPECTED SPEAKERS WHO SPOKE IN FAVOUR OF WOMEN'S EDUCATION WHENEVER THEY COULD. BUT -
YOU KNOW, I CAN'T FORGET EVERYTHING THAT WE HAVE SEEN IN ALL THESE YEARS. THE SO-CALLED HOLY MEN, THEIR SOLUTIONS TO PROBLEMS, THE WAY WE WERE TREATED....
I KNOW. IT BOTHERS ME TOO. ALL OF THEM WERE JUST LOOKING FOR WAYS TO LINE THEIR OWN POCKETS. NOT ONE PERSON HELPED US.

WELL, THEY WERE TOO BUSY HELPING THEMSELVES!
HAHAHA! QUITE RIGHT, BIPIN!
IT WAS SRINIVASA'S FRIEND, BIPIN BEHARI MEDHAVI, A MAN FROM WHAT WAS THEN CONSIDERED A LOW CASTE WHO HAD STUDIED LAW.

THOUGH COMFORTABLE NOW, THE YEARS OF WANDERING AND SEVERE STARVATION HAD TAKEN A TOLL ON SRINIVASA'S HEALTH. TO RAMABAI'S SORROW, HE TOO PASSED AWAY.
MY POOR BROTHER! YOU WERE MY ONLY COMPANION AND NOW YOU TOO ARE GONE.
RAMA WAS NOW COMPLETELY ALONE. SHE WAS 22, UNMARRIED AND WITHOUT ANY FAMILY.

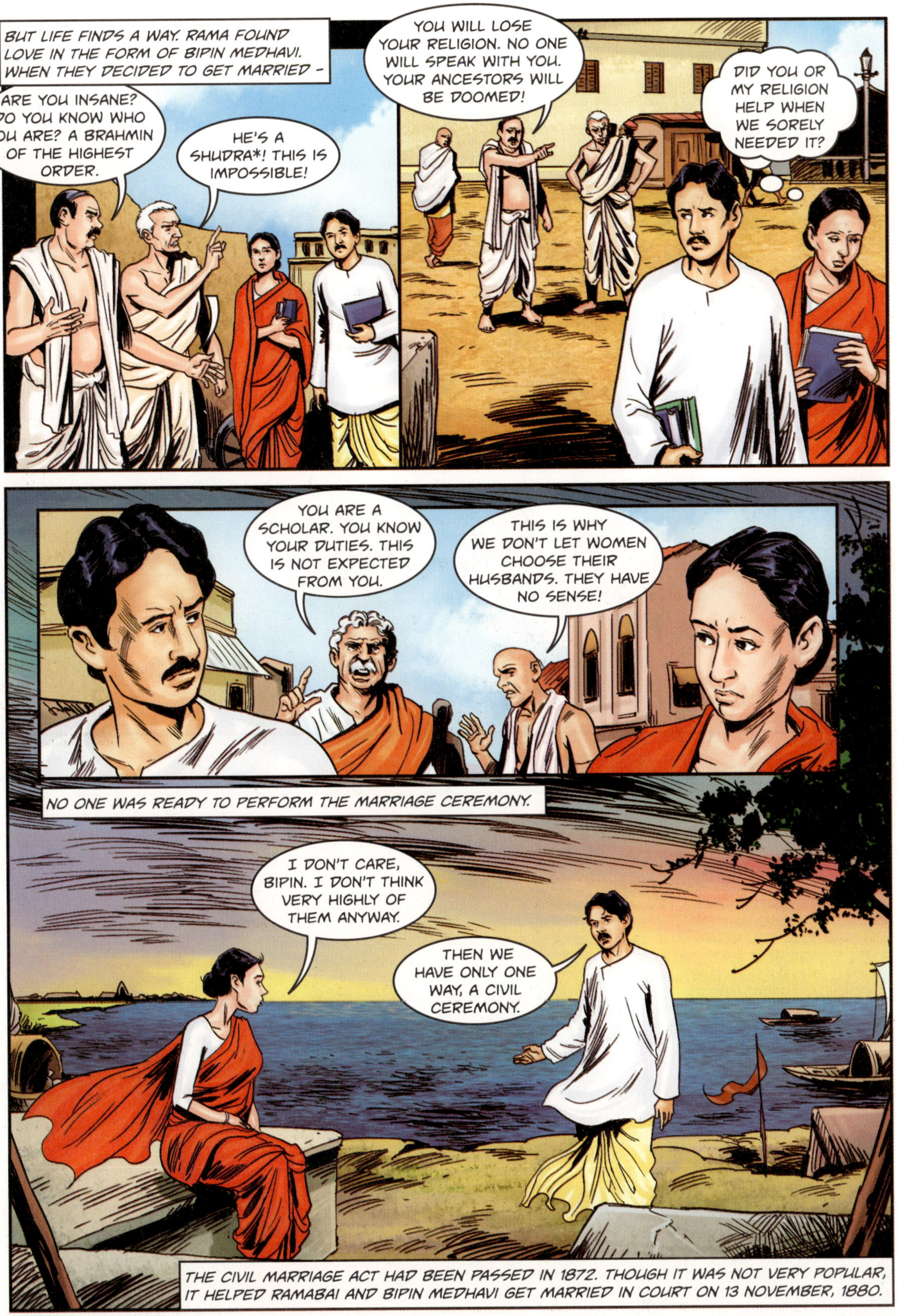

YOU ARE A SCHOLAR. YOU KNOW YOUR DUTIES. THIS IS NOT EXPECTED FROM YOU.

THIS IS WHY WE DON'T LET WOMEN CHOOSE THEIR HUSBANDS. THEY HAVE NO SENSE!

NO ONE WAS READY TO PERFORM THE MARRIAGE CEREMONY.

I DON'T CARE, BIPIN. I DON'T THINK VERY HIGHLY OF THEM ANYWAY.

THEN WE HAVE ONLY ONE WAY, A CIVIL CEREMONY.

THE CIVIL MARRIAGE ACT HAD BEEN PASSED IN 1872. THOUGH IT WAS NOT VERY POPULAR, IT HELPED RAMABAI AND BIPIN MEDHAVI GET MARRIED IN COURT ON 13 NOVEMBER, 1880.

*NAME OF A LOWER CASTE

*A CITY IN WEST BENGAL
^READ HER STORY ON PAGE 21

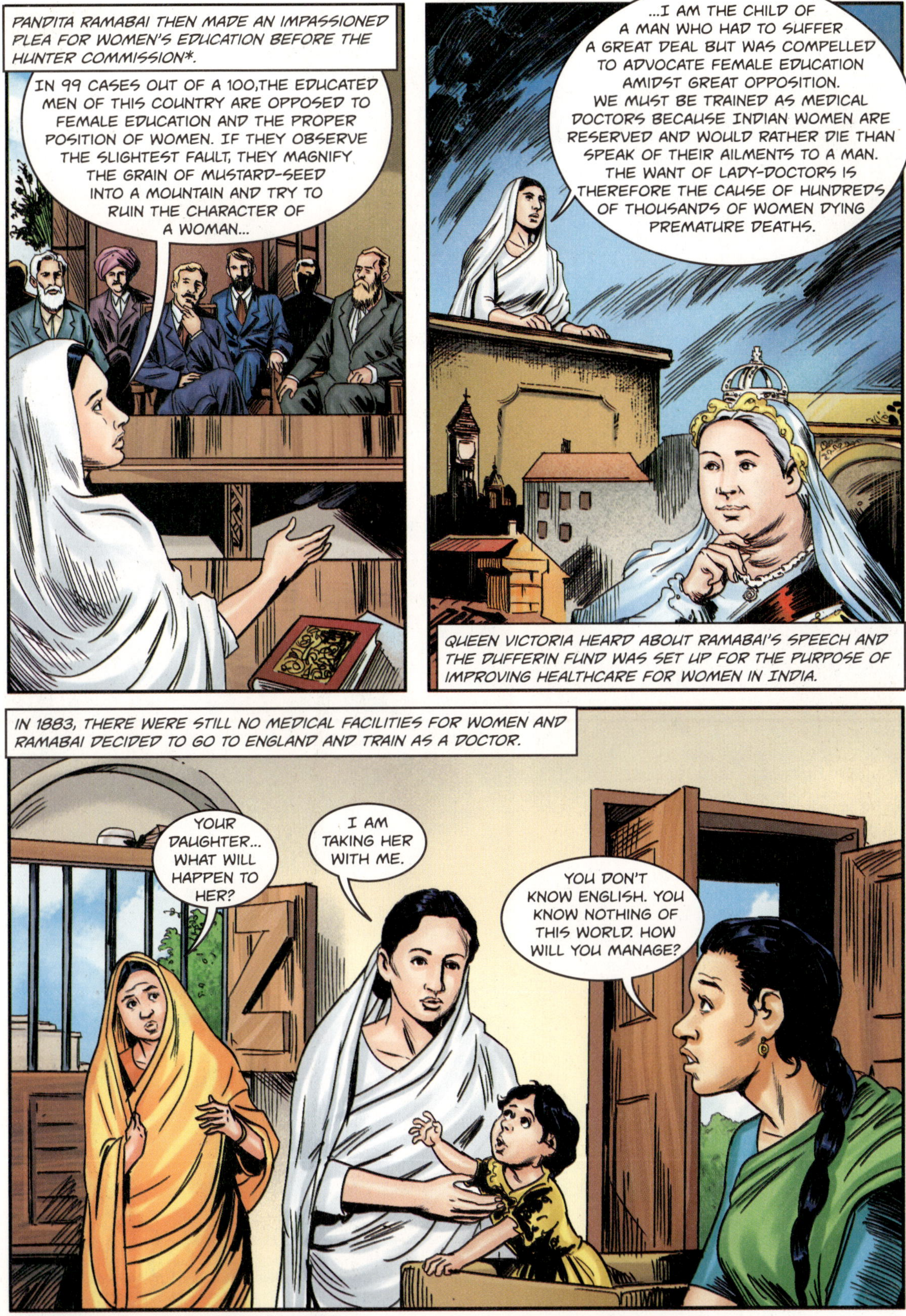

PANDITA RAMABAI THEN MADE AN IMPASSIONED PLEA FOR WOMEN'S EDUCATION BEFORE THE HUNTER COMMISSION*.

IN 99 CASES OUT OF A 100,THE EDUCATED MEN OF THIS COUNTRY ARE OPPOSED TO FEMALE EDUCATION AND THE PROPER POSITION OF WOMEN. IF THEY OBSERVE THE SLIGHTEST FAULT, THEY MAGNIFY THE GRAIN OF MUSTARD-SEED INTO A MOUNTAIN AND TRY TO RUIN THE CHARACTER OF A WOMAN...

QUEEN VICTORIA HEARD ABOUT RAMABAI'S SPEECH AND THE DUFFERIN FUND WAS SET UP FOR THE PURPOSE OF IMPROVING HEALTHCARE FOR WOMEN IN INDIA.

IN 1883, THERE WERE STILL NO MEDICAL FACILITIES FOR WOMEN AND RAMABAI DECIDED TO GO TO ENGLAND AND TRAIN AS A DOCTOR.

YOUR DAUGHTER... WHAT WILL HAPPEN TO HER?

I AM TAKING HER WITH ME.

YOU DON'T KNOW ENGLISH. YOU KNOW NOTHING OF THIS WORLD. HOW WILL YOU MANAGE?

*THE INDIAN EDUCATION COMMISSION SET UP IN 1882 BY LORD RIPON, VICEROY OF BRITISH INDIA

BUT RAMABAI WAS DETERMINED AND IN APRIL, 1883, SHE SAILED FOR ENGLAND WITH MANORAMA. SHE WAS OFFERED SHELTER BY THE ANGLICAN COMMUNITY OF ST MARY THE VIRGIN AT WANTAGE, WHERE SHE STAYED AND STUDIED FOR A WHILE.
OH MY DEAR, BE STRONG. I'M HOLDING YOU.
THE WOMEN HERE ARE SO KIND TO EACH OTHER... ALWAYS READY TO HELP. WHY DO I NOT SEE THAT IN INDIA?

IS IT BECAUSE IN INDIA, WE DO NOT HAVE A COMMUNITY OF OUR OWN AS SUCH? BECAUSE WE OURSELVES BELIEVE THAT WE ARE WEAK AND HELPLESS?

BY THIS TIME, RAMABAI'S OWN QUESTIONS ABOUT HER FAITH HAD BEGUN TO TROUBLE HER.
MY LIFE AND MY PARENTS' LIVES BEFORE ME HAVE BEEN OFFERED IN THE SERVICE OF MY FAITH AND YET MY RELIGION DOES NOT PROVIDE ANY COMFORT TO ME. IT HAS ONLY CREATED OBSTACLES FOR ME AT EVERY STEP.

ONE DAY -
PANDITA! PANDITA RAMABAI!

PANDITA! DID YOU NOT HEAR ME?
HUH?
RAMABAI HAD NOT HEARD HER. SHE WAS BECOMING DEAF! AS A RESULT, SHE HAD TO STOP STUDYING MEDICINE AND TAKE UP ENGLISH AND SCIENCE.

PANDITA RAMABAI HAD SLOWLY BEEN DRAWN TO CHRISTIAN PHILOSOPHY OVER THE YEARS. IN SEPTEMBER, 1883, SHE AND HER DAUGHTER CONVERTED TO CHRISTIANITY.

ALL OF INDIA WAS AGHAST!
WE CANNOT CONDEMN HER ENOUGH! SHE HAS REBELLED AT EVERY TURN. FIRST SHE STUDIED, THEN SHE MARRIED A MAN OF A LOWER CASTE AND REFUSED TO LIVE A QUIET AND SACRIFICING LIFE LIKE EVERY SELF-RESPECTING WIDOW. AND NOW THIS!

MY CONVERSION HAS NOTHING TO DO WITH SOCIETY. ALL MY LIFE, I HAVE FELT THE PRESENCE OF A KIND AND LOVING GOD. NOW I BELIEVE I HAVE FOUND HIM.

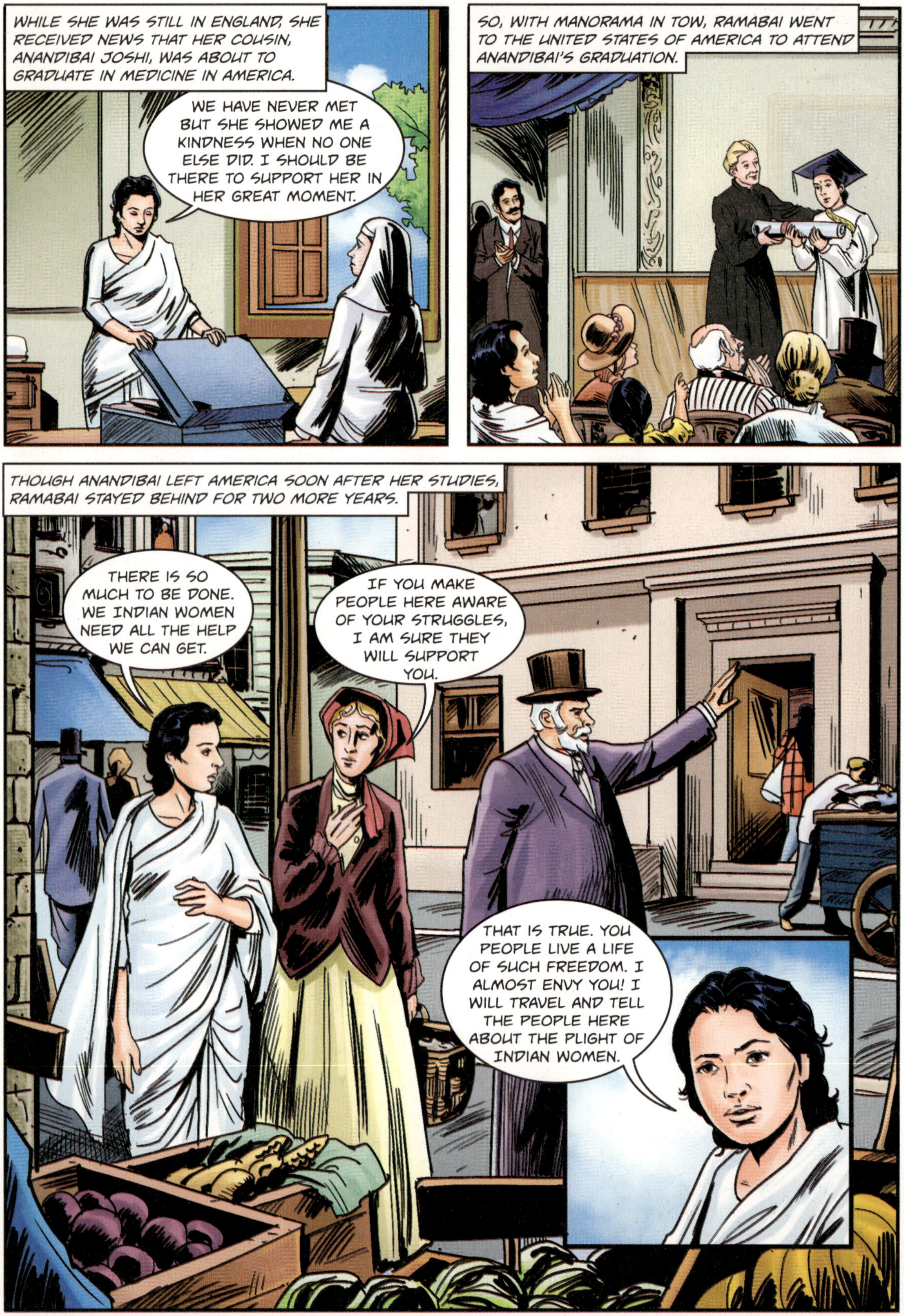

THOUGH ANANDIBAI LEFT AMERICA SOON AFTER HER STUDIES, RAMABAI STAYED BEHIND FOR TWO MORE YEARS.

THERE IS SO MUCH TO BE DONE. WE INDIAN WOMEN NEED ALL THE HELP WE CAN GET.

IF YOU MAKE PEOPLE HERE AWARE OF YOUR STRUGGLES, I AM SURE THEY WILL SUPPORT YOU.

THAT IS TRUE. YOU PEOPLE LIVE A LIFE OF SUCH FREEDOM. I ALMOST ENVY YOU! I WILL TRAVEL AND TELL THE PEOPLE HERE ABOUT THE PLIGHT OF INDIAN WOMEN.

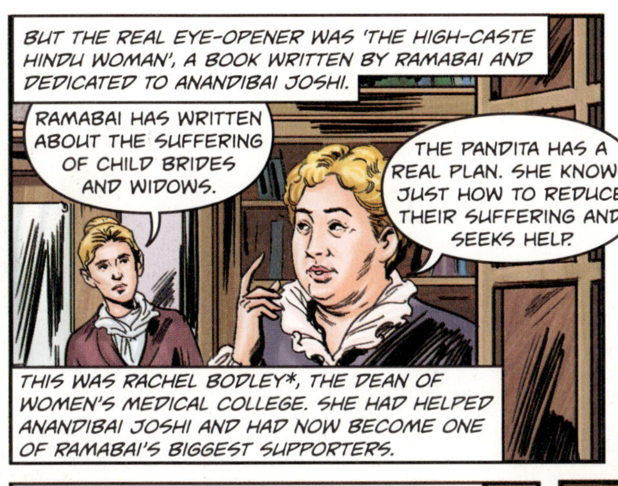

RAMABAI CALLED FOR A LIBRARY IN EACH HOUSE THROUGH WHICH THE GIRLS WOULD EDUCATE THEMSELVES, WITH THE HELP OF TEACHERS, IN HISTORY, SCIENCE, ART AND LITERATURE.

SHE SAW THE GIRLS GETTING ACCESS TO EDUCATION AND OPENING THEIR EYES AND EARS TO KNOWLEDGE.

*RACHEL BODLEY WROTE THE ORIGINAL INTRODUCTION TO RAMABAI'S 'THE HIGH-CASTE HINDU WOMAN'.

IMPRESSED BY HER VISION, MANY PEOPLE CAME FORWARD WITH DONATIONS. THE 'AMERICAN RAMABAI ASSOCIATION' WAS FORMED AND IN 1889, RAMABAI WAS ON HER WAY HOME WITH THE MEANS TO PUT HER PLANS INTO ACTION.
INDIA, MY BELOVED COUNTRY! WHAT KIND OF RECEPTION WILL YOU GIVE ME? WILL YOU SUPPORT ME OR WILL YOU ABANDON ME, THINKING THAT I HAVE ABANDONED YOU?

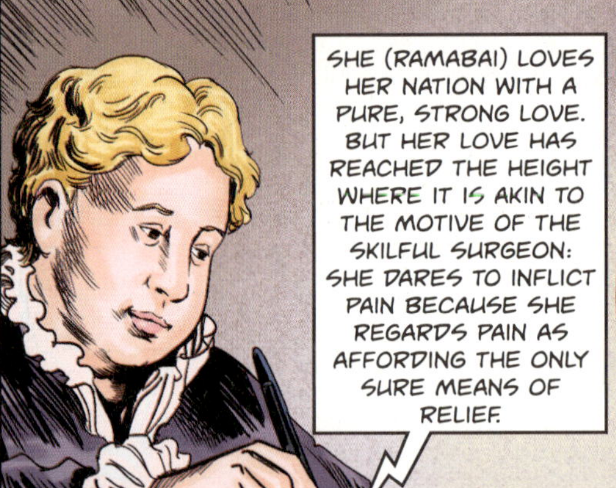
IN INDIA, THE REACTION TO HER BOOK HAD BEEN DIVIDED. WHILE MOST SAW IT AS A BETRAYAL, A FEW RECOGNISED THE NEED FOR IT. AS RACHEL BODLEY HAD SAID IN HER INTRODUCTION TO THE BOOK -
SHE (RAMABAI) LOVES HER NATION WITH A PURE, STRONG LOVE. BUT HER LOVE HAS REACHED THE HEIGHT WHERE IT IS AKIN TO THE MOTIVE OF THE SKILFUL SURGEON: SHE DARES TO INFLICT PAIN BECAUSE SHE REGARDS PAIN AS AFFORDING THE ONLY SURE MEANS OF RELIEF.

BACK IN INDIA, SHE SET TO WORK IMMEDIATELY.
I WANT TO BUILD A HOME... A SAFE HOME WHERE WIDOWS CAN COME AND LIVE A RESPECTABLE AND INDEPENDENT LIFE.

'SHARADA SADAN'- HOME OF LEARNING. CONGRATULATIONS, RAMABAI! YOU HAVE ACHIEVED THE IMPOSSIBLE.
WE WILL GIVE WIDOWS A PROPER FORMAL EDUCATION HERE AND ALSO VOCATIONAL TRAINING.

RAMABAI SOON SHIFTED SHARADA SADAN FROM BOMBAY* TO POONA WHERE SHE FELT THERE WAS A GREATER NEED FOR HELP. BUT –
RAMABAI, MANY PEOPLE ARE PROTESTING THAT YOU WILL TURN HINDU WIDOWS INTO CHRISTIANS.
LET THEM. I AM HERE BECAUSE THERE ARE MORE WIDOWS HERE THAT NEED MY HELP. THAT IS THE TRUTH.

SHARADA SADAN BROUGHT HAPPINESS AND A SENSE OF PURPOSE INTO THE LIVES OF MANY WOMEN WHO HAD FELT HOPELESS BEFORE. MANY STUDIED THERE AND WENT ON TO TEACH OUTSIDE AND EVEN OPEN SCHOOLS OF THEIR OWN. SOME BECAME NURSES, HOUSEKEEPERS AND ARTISANS. A FEW YEARS LATER –
RAMABAI, A HUNDRED ACRES OF FARMLAND OUTSIDE POONA IS AVAILABLE FOR A VERY REASONABLE PRICE. SHOULD WE BUY IT?
YES, I HAVE BEEN THINKING OF EXPANDING. THERE IS HARDLY ANY SPACE LEFT HERE NOW.
THAT WAS TRUE. SHARADA SADAN WAS PACKED TO THE BRIM WITH WIDOWS AND UNMARRIED WOMEN WHO HAD SOUGHT REFUGE THERE.

RAMABAI UNDERTOOK ANOTHER ROUND OF SUCCESSFUL FUNDING AND, IN 1896, THE 'MUKTI MISSION' WAS SET UP ON THE FARMLAND IN KEDGAON. IT HAD FACILITIES FOR EVERYONE – HINDU WIDOWS, WOMEN FROM OTHER COMMUNITIES, BLIND WOMEN, OLD WOMEN AND CHILDREN COULD ALL COME HERE TO LEARN AND LIVE A DECENT LIFE.
MUKTI MISSION
KEDGAON

THAT SAME YEAR, ANOTHER TERRIBLE FAMINE HIT THE COUNTRY.

WILL MORE CHILDREN FACE THE SAME CALAMITIES THAT I DID? IN THE NAME OF MY FAMILY, I MUST HELP!
FRANTIC WITH WORRY, RAMABAI RUSHED TO ALL THE AFFLICTED REGIONS, RESCUING ANYONE WHO NEEDED HELP.

*NOW MUMBAI

*MOTHER IN MARATHI

BUT GRIEF WAS TO COME KNOCKING AT HER DOOR ONCE AGAIN. THE VERY NEXT YEAR, MANORAMA SUDDENLY PASSED AWAY. ALREADY ILL WITH SEPTIC BRONCHITIS, THIS WAS A SHOCK THAT RAMABAI COULD NOT RECOVER FROM AND A FEW MONTHS LATER, ON 5 APRIL, 1922, SHE TOO BREATHED HER LAST.

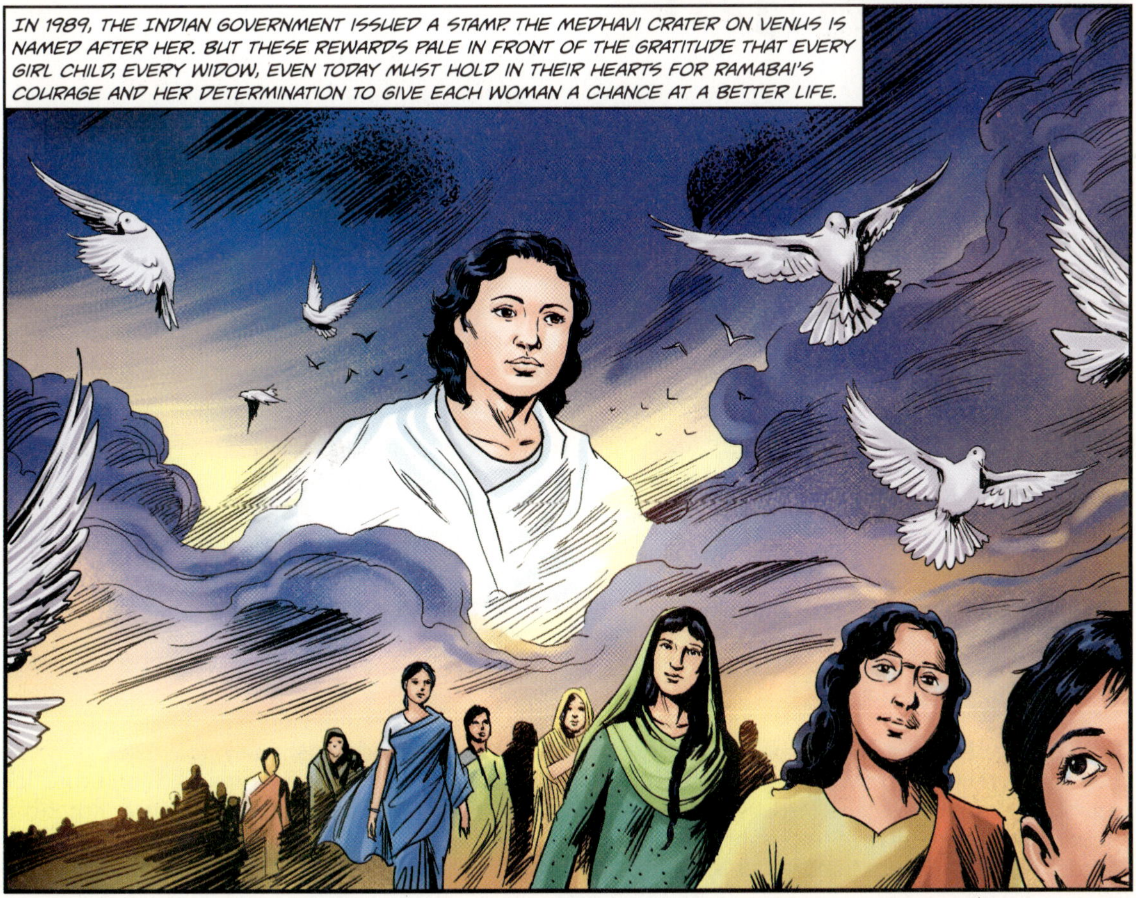

IN 1989, THE INDIAN GOVERNMENT ISSUED A STAMP. THE MEDHAVI CRATER ON VENUS IS NAMED AFTER HER. BUT THESE REWARDS PALE IN FRONT OF THE GRATITUDE THAT EVERY GIRL CHILD, EVERY WIDOW, EVEN TODAY MUST HOLD IN THEIR HEARTS FOR RAMABAI'S COURAGE AND HER DETERMINATION TO GIVE EACH WOMAN A CHANCE AT A BETTER LIFE.

Ramabai Ranade

Social reformer

Ramabai Ranade was one of India's earliest social reformers and women's rights activists. She tried to make women educated and self-reliant while living within the norms of society.

Born in 1863 into a conservative family, Ramabai's life changed when she was married at the age of 11. Her husband Mahadev Govind Ranade was 21 years her senior and extremely well-educated. He started educating young Ramabai.

When she was old enough, Ramabai started taking a keen interest in her husband's activities as a social reformer. She became the first Indian woman to address a public gathering when she was invited to be the chief guest at Nasik High School, Maharashtra. Though extremely nervous, Ramabai managed to speak simply but effectively.

Ramabai formed the Hindu Ladies Social and Literary Club in Bombay where she encouraged education for women. She also trained them in public speaking, general knowledge, tailoring and other skills to make them self-sufficient. In 1886, along with her husband and a few others, Ramabai established Huzurpaga, the first high school for girls in Poona.

In 1901, she suffered a major setback when her husband passed away. She put aside her personal feelings of loss and threw herself into her work. She began helping women and children in prison and patients in hospitals. She fought for widow remarriage and against untouchability and child marriage.

In 1908, social reformers B.M. Malabari and Dayaram Gidumal founded Seva Sadan. They wanted to establish a refuge for women and educate them to assert their place in society. The ideal person to help in this job was Ramabai Ranade. Under her leadership, Seva Sadan gave widows and abandoned girls a new lease of life. The following year, Ramabai opened a branch in Poona.

She campaigned extensively to make primary education compulsory for girls and to secure for women the right to vote. By the time Ramabai died in 1924, there were more than a thousand girls living in Seva Sadan.

Anandibai Joshi - First lady doctor

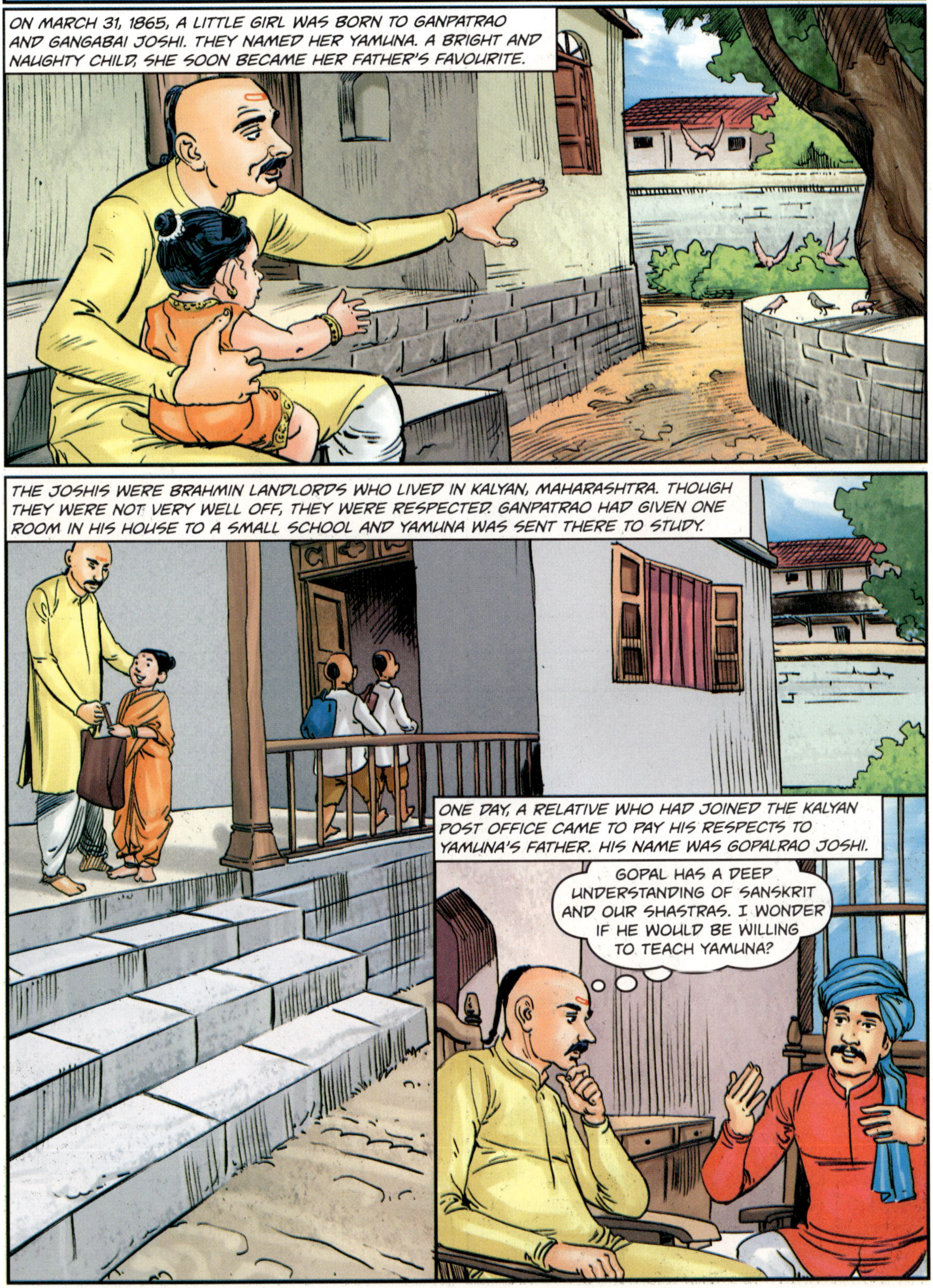

THE JOSHIS WERE BRAHMIN LANDLORDS WHO LIVED IN KALYAN, MAHARASHTRA. THOUGH THEY WERE NOT VERY WELL OFF, THEY WERE RESPECTED. GANPATRAO HAD GIVEN ONE ROOM IN HIS HOUSE TO A SMALL SCHOOL AND YAMUNA WAS SENT THERE TO STUDY.

ONE DAY, A RELATIVE WHO HAD JOINED THE KALYAN POST OFFICE CAME TO PAY HIS RESPECTS TO YAMUNA'S FATHER. HIS NAME WAS GOPALRAO JOSHI.

GOPAL HAS A DEEP UNDERSTANDING OF SANSKRIT AND OUR SHASTRAS. I WONDER IF HE WOULD BE WILLING TO TEACH YAMUNA?

*CHILD MARRIAGE WAS COMMON IN THOSE DAYS. IT WAS ABOLISHED IN 1929 UNDER INDIAN LAW.

WHEN ANANDI WAS ELEVEN, GOPALRAO GOT POSTED OUT OF KALYAN. IT WAS THEN THAT HE AND ANANDI SET UP HOME AND BEGAN THEIR NEW LIFE TOGETHER. IT WAS A MOST UNUSUAL MARRIAGE!
ANANDI, DID YOU DO YOUR HOMEWORK?
NOT YET. I WAS HELPING GRANDMOTHER WITH THE HOUSEWORK.

HOW MANY TIMES HAVE I TOLD YOU THAT THE HOUSEWORK CAN BE DONE BY ANYBODY BUT NO ONE CAN DO YOUR HOMEWORK FOR YOU! THAT MUST BE DONE FIRST!
HE'S A STRANGE FELLOW! SCOLDING HER FOR DOING THE HOUSEWORK! MOST WIVES GET SCOLDED FOR NOT DOING IT.
ANANDI'S GRANDMOTHER HAD ACCOMPANIED HER TO HELP SET UP THE HOUSE.

GOPAL ALSO SHOCKED HIS NEIGHBOURS BY TAKING ANANDI OUT FOR LONG WALKS WITH HIM.
SO YOU SEE, ANANDI, IT IS IMPORTANT TO LEARN MARATHI AND SANSKRIT BUT YOU MUST ALSO LEARN ENGLISH TO KEEP UP WITH THE TIMES.

HAS HE NO SHAME? HOW CAN HE TAKE HIS WIFE OUT LIKE THAT?
HE IS ACTUALLY EDUCATING HER? WHAT IS WRONG WITH HIM?

IN THE NEXT FEW YEARS, GOPALRAO WAS POSTED TO DIFFERENT PARTS OF INDIA BUT HE MADE SURE THAT ANANDI'S EDUCATION NEVER STOPPED, WHETHER AT HOME OR AT SCHOOL. ONCE -
THEY ASKED ME TO READ THE BIBLE IN SCHOOL! I SAID NO AND WALKED OUT. I'M NEVER GOING BACK.
HA HA! THERE IS NOTHING WRONG IN READING THE BIBLE, ANANDI!

GASP! YOU WANT ME TO BECOME A CHRISTIAN?
HOW WILL READING A BOOK MAKE YOU A CHRISTIAN? IT'S GOOD TO READ OTHER PEOPLE'S BOOKS. YOU LEARN SO MUCH.

I HATE WALKING TO SCHOOL. MY FEET HURT SO MUCH AND EVERYBODY STARES!
THE STARES, YOU JUST HAVE TO GET USED TO. BUT HERE...

...THESE WILL HELP YOUR FEET.
SHOES! SOCKS!
IN THOSE DAYS BRAHMIN WOMEN DID NOT WEAR SHOES AS THEY WERE CONSIDERED 'FOREIGN' AND, THEREFORE, IMPURE.

THE NEXT MORNING -
LET THEM STARE. THESE SHOES ARE COMFORTABLE AND I AM DOING NOTHING WRONG.
GASP!
WHAT IS SHE DOING?
ANANDI WAS NOW GROWING CONFIDENT ENOUGH TO NOT LET THE STARES AFFECT HER TOO MUCH.
WHEN SHE WAS JUST 14, A SON WAS BORN TO THEM BUT HE DIED A FEW DAYS LATER.
SOB SOB SOB
HE DIED BECAUSE WE COULDN'T GET HIM TREATED! BECAUSE I COULDN'T GET TREATED!
ANANDI'S SON HAD DIED BECAUSE, AS A WOMAN, SHE COULD NOT GO TO A MALE DOCTOR.
THIS WAS THE CASE WITH THOUSANDS OF WOMEN AT THAT TIME. MANY DIED EARLY BECAUSE NO ONE HAD THOUGHT OF A SOLUTION. SUDDENLY -
NO MORE! NO MORE SUFFERING! I AM GOING TO BECOME A DOCTOR.
A WHAT?
AT A TIME WHEN INDIAN WOMEN WERE RARELY EVEN EDUCATED, ANANDI'S WORDS WERE STARTLING!

*A PROFESSIONAL COURSE WHERE A PERSON CAN TRAIN IN THE CARE OF PREGNANCY, CHILDBIRTH AND OTHER RELATED PROBLEMS

^TO OFFICIALLY REMOVE A PERSON FROM THE COMMUNITY HE OR SHE BELONGS TO

IN SEPTEMBER, 1878, GOPAL WROTE TO A PRESBYTERIAN MISSIONARY IN KOLHAPUR DISCUSSING HIS BELIEF IN WOMEN'S EDUCATION AND STATING HIS WIFE'S WISH TO BECOME A DOCTOR. HE ADDED -

If you can help us, I will be glad to live in America and support my wife.

THIS LETTER FOUND ITS WAY TO THE 'MISSIONARY REVIEW' PUBLISHED IN PRINCETON, USA, WHERE IT WAS ACCOMPANIED BY A SERIES OF COMMENTS FROM THE EDITOR COMPLETELY DISCOURAGING THE PROJECT.
"AN UNCONVERTED HINDU SEEKING OUR HELP TO STUDY IN THE USA? WE MUST FIRST HELP OUR FELLOW CHRISTIANS TO PROGRESS IN THIS WORLD."
GOPAL AND ANANDI WOULD NEVER HAVE KNOWN ANYTHING ABOUT THIS IF DESTINY HAD NOT PLAYED A VERY STRANGE HAND.

TWO YEARS LATER AND THOUSANDS OF MILES AWAY IN NEW JERSEY, USA, AS THEODICIA CARPENTER SAT WAITING FOR HER DENTAL APPOINTMENT –
WHAT A LOVELY LETTER! WHO IS THIS COUPLE?
SHE HAD CHANCED UPON GOPAL'S LETTER IN THE MISSIONARY REVIEW.
WHAT A FORWARD THINKING, SUPPORTIVE MAN. HOW DOES IT MATTER THAT THEY DON'T WANT TO BECOME CHRISTIANS?
SHE COPIED DOWN GOPAL'S ADDRESS FROM THE MAGAZINE.

OVER THE NEXT FEW DAYS, SHE FOUND THAT SHE COULD NOT STOP THINKING ABOUT GOPAL AND ANANDI.
THAT POOR GIRL...JUST 14 AND LOST HER SON. NOW SHE WANTS TO BECOME A DOCTOR. HER HUSBAND IS TRYING TO HELP HER BUT THEY JUST DON'T HAVE THE OPPORTUNITIES THAT WE HAVE.
ARE YOU SAYING THAT YOU WANT TO HELP THEM? YOU DON'T KNOW ANYTHING ABOUT THEM. THEY COULD BE BARBARIANS!

HER LETTER WAS SO WARM AND KIND THAT ANANDI FOUND HERSELF REPLYING IMMEDIATELY. THUS BEGAN A SERIES OF EXCHANGES THAT HELPED BOTH WOMEN DEVELOP A STRONG BOND WITH EACH OTHER. MRS CARPENTER ALSO GOT A GLIMPSE INTO ANANDI'S MIND.

*We Indian women suffer from innumerable small diseases, unnoticed until they grow serious...fifty per cent die in the prime of their youth, of disease arising partly through ignorance and their unwillingness to communicate, and partly through the carelessness of their guardians or husbands.**

THOUGH ANANDI COULD NOT SPEAK ENGLISH FLUENTLY, SHE COULD WRITE IT BEAUTIFULLY.

*THE LANGUAGE OF THE LETTER HAS BEEN SIMPLIFIED.

*ANANDI HAD STARTED ADDRESSING MRS CARPENTER AS HER 'AUNT'.

"OUR ANCIENT INDIAN LADIES WERE VERY WISE, COURAGEOUS AND BENEVOLENT, AND ENDURANCE WAS THEIR BADGE. LET IT BE MY BADGE ALSO. LET ME TRY TO DO MY DUTY, WHETHER I BE VICTOR OR VICTIM."
LOOK AT HER THOUGHTS. I CAN'T BELIEVE THIS CHILD IS NOT YET 18!
IN INDIA, HOWEVER, PEOPLE SHOUTED AT THE COUPLE AND CALLED THEM NAMES. THEY WERE SUBJECTED TO THE MOST HUMILIATING COMMENTS AND CHOICEST ABUSES.
HAVE YOU LOST ALL YOUR SELF-RESPECT?
EVEN THE FEAR OF EXCOMMUNICATION ISN'T ENOUGH FOR THESE TWO!
THEIR HOUSE IN SERAMPORE WAS SURROUNDED BY ANGRY PEOPLE AT ALL HOURS OF THE DAY.
ON 24 FEBRUARY, 1883, ANANDI ADDRESSED A PUBLIC GATHERING AT SERAMPORE COLLEGE HALL.
I WANT TO GO TO AMERICA BECAUSE I WISH TO STUDY MEDICINE. THERE IS A GROWING NEED FOR HINDU LADY DOCTORS IN INDIA AND I VOLUNTEER TO QUALIFY MYSELF AS ONE. WHY SHOULD I BE CAST OUT OF MY COMMUNITY WHEN I HAVE DETERMINED TO LIVE THERE EXACTLY AS I DO HERE? I WILL GO AS A HINDU AND COME BACK HERE TO LIVE AS A HINDU...
THE AUDIENCE LISTENED IN STUNNED SILENCE.

...A MAN OR A WOMAN WHO WISHES TO ACT DOES NOT LOOK AT INEVITABLE EVILS THAT MAY CRUSH HIM OR HER. WHEN THEY HAPPEN, THEY MUST BE ENDURED. YOU ASK ME WHY I WANT TO DO SOMETHING THAT NO OTHER WOMAN HAS DONE BEFORE. THIS I CAN ONLY SAY, IF ANYTHING SEEMS BEST FOR ALL MANKIND, EACH ONE OF US MUST TRY TO BRING IT ABOUT.

ACCORDING TO MANU*, THE DESERTION OF DUTY IS AN UNPARDONABLE SIN. OUR ANCESTORS HAD NO SUCH THOUGHTS IN THEIR HEADS. TO STAY AWAY FROM DUTY BECAUSE WE FEAR FAILURE OR SUFFERING IS NOT RIGHT. WE MUST TRY. THE GREATER THE DIFFICULTY, THE GREATER MUST BE OUR COURAGE.

IN THE AUDIENCE WAS MR H.E.M. JAMES, THE DIRECTOR GENERAL OF THE POST OFFICES OF INDIA. SO IMPRESSED WAS HE BY ANANDI'S WORDS THAT HE DONATED A HUNDRED RUPEES TOWARDS HER JOURNEY AND ASKED OTHERS TO CONTRIBUTE. THE 'JAMES FUND' WAS CREATED TO HELP ANANDI PAY HER TUITION FEES IN AMERICA.

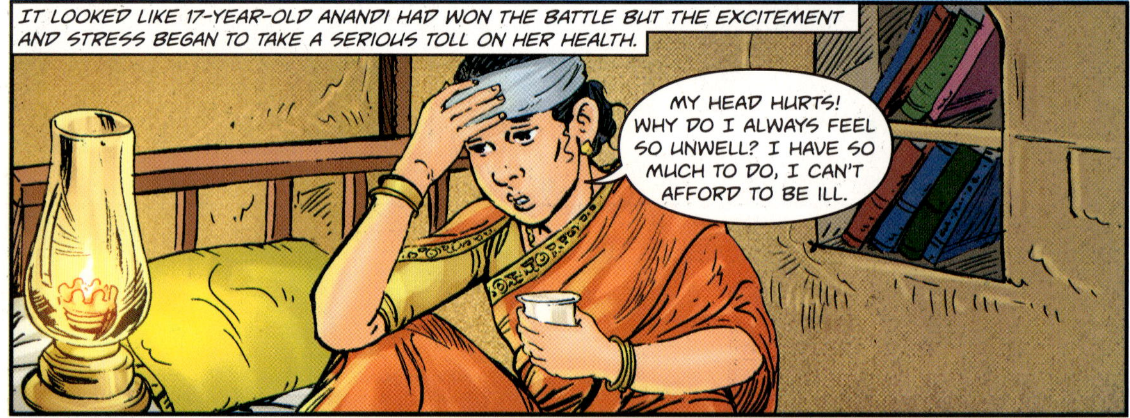

*THE FIRST MAN WHO WROTE THE MANUSMRITI, A BOOK ON HINDU CODES AND LAWS.

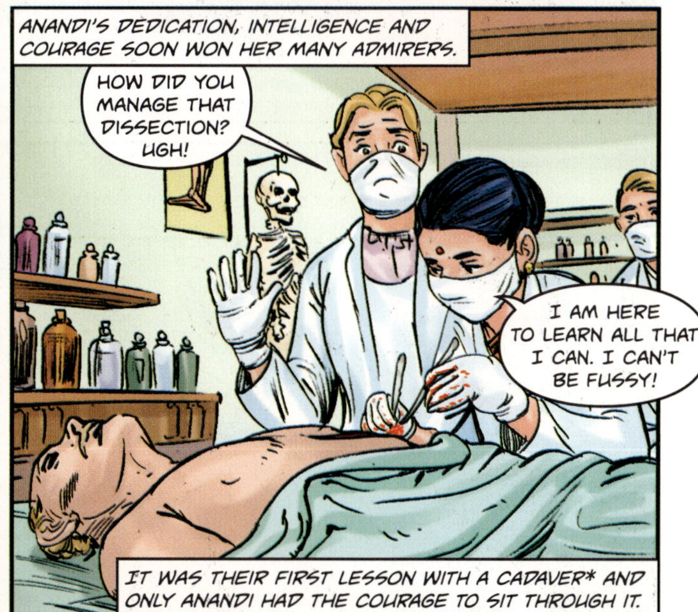

*A DEAD BODY USED BY MEDICAL STUDENTS FOR DISSECTION

THE YEARS FLEW BY AND SOON IT WAS TIME FOR HER TO GRADUATE. ANANDI'S COUSIN PANDITA RAMABAI^ AND GOPALRAO WERE PRESENT FOR HER GRADUATION CEREMONY. WHEN SHE WENT TO RECEIVE HER CERTIFICATE, THE ENTIRE HALL GAVE HER A STANDING OVATION!

CLAP! CLAP! CLAP! CLAP! CLAP!

ANANDI'S THESIS WAS ON 'OBSTETRICS AMONG THE HINDU ARYANS' WHICH WON HER HIGH HONOURS. SHE WAS NOW DR ANANDIBAI JOSHI! EVEN QUEEN VICTORIA SENT HER A CONGRATULATORY MESSAGE.

*MRS CAROLINE DALL BECAME A CLOSE FRIEND AND WAS ANANDI'S FIRST BIOGRAPHER.
^STORY ON PAGE 3

YOU HAVE DONE IT, ANANDI. YOU CAN STRAIGHTAWAY START TREATING OTHER WOMEN.
AND I CAN TEACH THEM TOO! OH, I AM SO HAPPY!

THOUGH SERIOUSLY ILL, ANANDI LEFT FOR INDIA IN OCTOBER, 1886, EXCITED TO PUT INTO PRACTICE ALL THAT SHE HAD LEARNT.
IT WAS A LONG AND DIFFICULT JOURNEY AND BY THE TIME SHE REACHED BOMBAY*, SHE WAS VERY ILL.

BOMBAY GAVE HER A HERO'S WELCOME! THE SAME PEOPLE WHO HAD ABUSED AND AVOIDED HER EARLIER NOW THRONGED THE SHORE TO CONGRATULATE HER.
SHE HAS DONE A TRULY GREAT THING. SHE SACRIFICED HER HOME LIFE SO THAT SHE MAY BRING COMFORT TO ALL THE WOMEN IN OUR COUNTRY.
WEL COME Dr. ANANDI BAI JOSHI

ANANDI NEVER MADE IT TO KOLHAPUR. SHE WAS SO ILL THAT SHE HAD TO STOP IN POONA. BULLETINS ABOUT HER HEALTH WERE ISSUED AND PEOPLE FERVENTLY PRAYED THAT SHE WOULD RECOVER SOON.

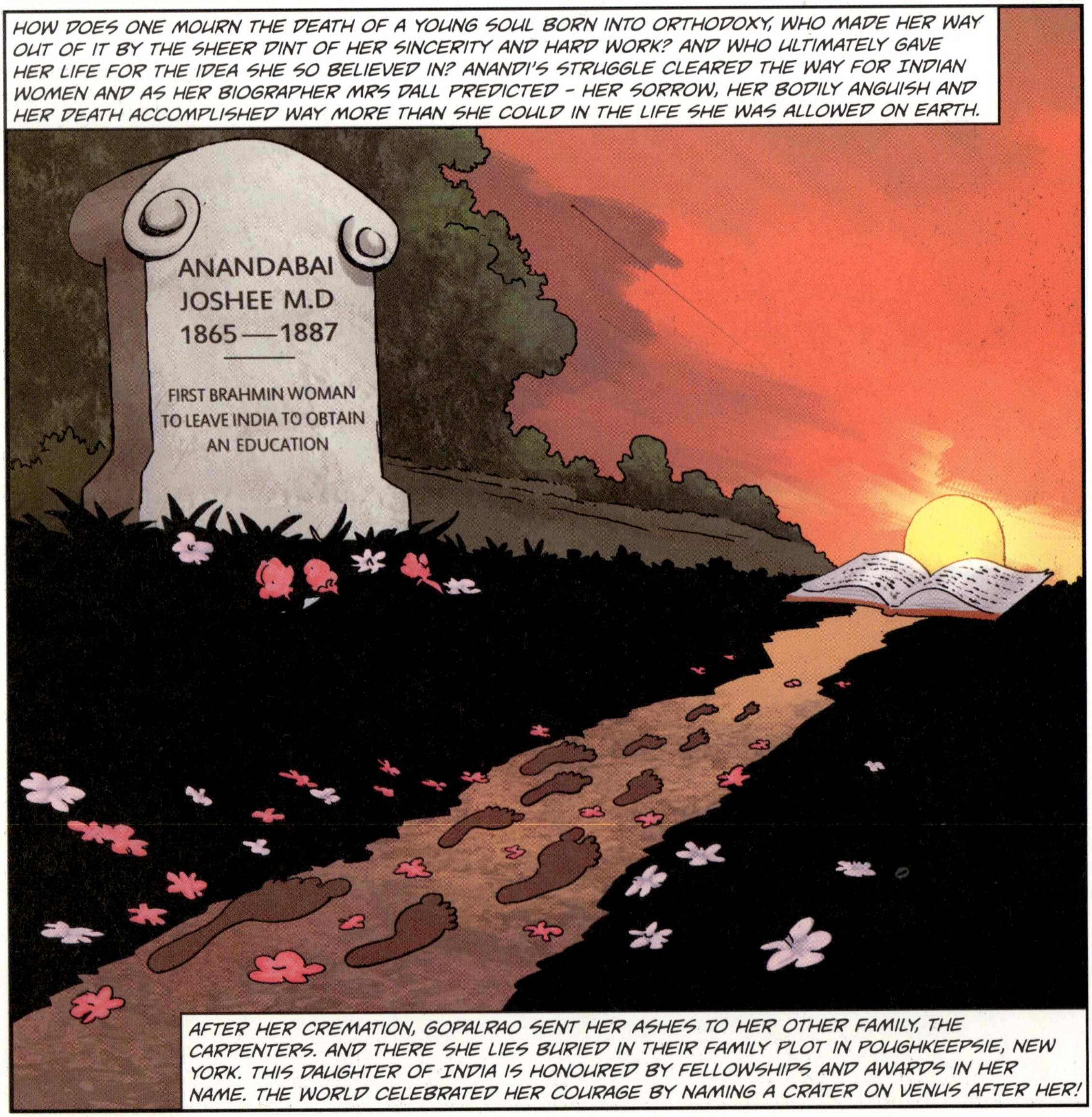

HOW DOES ONE MOURN THE DEATH OF A YOUNG SOUL BORN INTO ORTHODOXY, WHO MADE HER WAY OUT OF IT BY THE SHEER DINT OF HER SINCERITY AND HARD WORK? AND WHO ULTIMATELY GAVE HER LIFE FOR THE IDEA SHE SO BELIEVED IN? ANANDI'S STRUGGLE CLEARED THE WAY FOR INDIAN WOMEN AND AS HER BIOGRAPHER MRS DALL PREDICTED - HER SORROW, HER BODILY ANGUISH AND HER DEATH ACCOMPLISHED WAY MORE THAN SHE COULD IN THE LIFE SHE WAS ALLOWED ON EARTH.

ANANDABAI JOSHEE M.D
1865 — 1887
FIRST BRAHMIN WOMAN TO LEAVE INDIA TO OBTAIN AN EDUCATION

AFTER HER CREMATION, GOPALRAO SENT HER ASHES TO HER OTHER FAMILY, THE CARPENTERS. AND THERE SHE LIES BURIED IN THEIR FAMILY PLOT IN POUGHKEEPSIE, NEW YORK. THIS DAUGHTER OF INDIA IS HONOURED BY FELLOWSHIPS AND AWARDS IN HER NAME. THE WORLD CELEBRATED HER COURAGE BY NAMING A CRATER ON VENUS AFTER HER!

Rukhmabai

Inspired the 'Age of Consent' Act

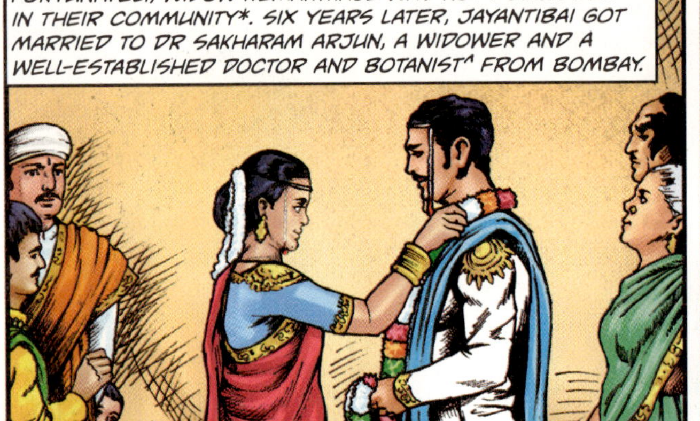

*THE SUTHAR OR CARPENTER COMMUNITY OF MAHARASHTRA

^HE WAS ONE OF THE FOUNDING MEMBERS OF THE BOMBAY NATURAL HISTORY SOCIETY (BNHS).

THOUGH RUKHMA'S STEPFATHER WAS BROAD-MINDED ENOUGH TO EDUCATE HER, HE STILL HAD TO FOLLOW THE CUSTOMS OF THAT TIME. THREE YEARS LATER –
RUKHMA IS ELEVEN NOW. WE SHOULD THINK OF GETTING HER MARRIED.
HMMM... I HAVE A DISTANT COUSIN WHOSE SON MIGHT BE ELIGIBLE...
...BUT IF SHE GETS MARRIED, RUKHMA WILL HAVE TO STOP GOING TO SCHOOL.
OBVIOUSLY! OF WHAT USE IS EDUCATION TO A MARRIED WOMAN?
SAKHARAM KNEW THAT RUKHMA ENJOYED LEARNING AND WAS KEEN ON CONTINUING HER EDUCATION. SO –
I WAS THINKING...IF THE BOY RUKHMA MARRIES WERE TO STAY HERE AFTER THE MARRIAGE, I COULD EDUCATE HIM TOO.
STAY HERE? OUR SON-IN-LAW WILL STAY IN OUR HOUSE! DO YOU KNOW WHAT YOU'RE SAYING?
THE BOY I HAVE IN MIND IS NOT VERY WELL OFF. IF HE CAN STAY HERE AND STUDY, IT WILL HELP HIM. BY THE TIME RUKHMA COMPLETES HER STUDIES, HE TOO WILL HAVE ACHIEVED SOMETHING.

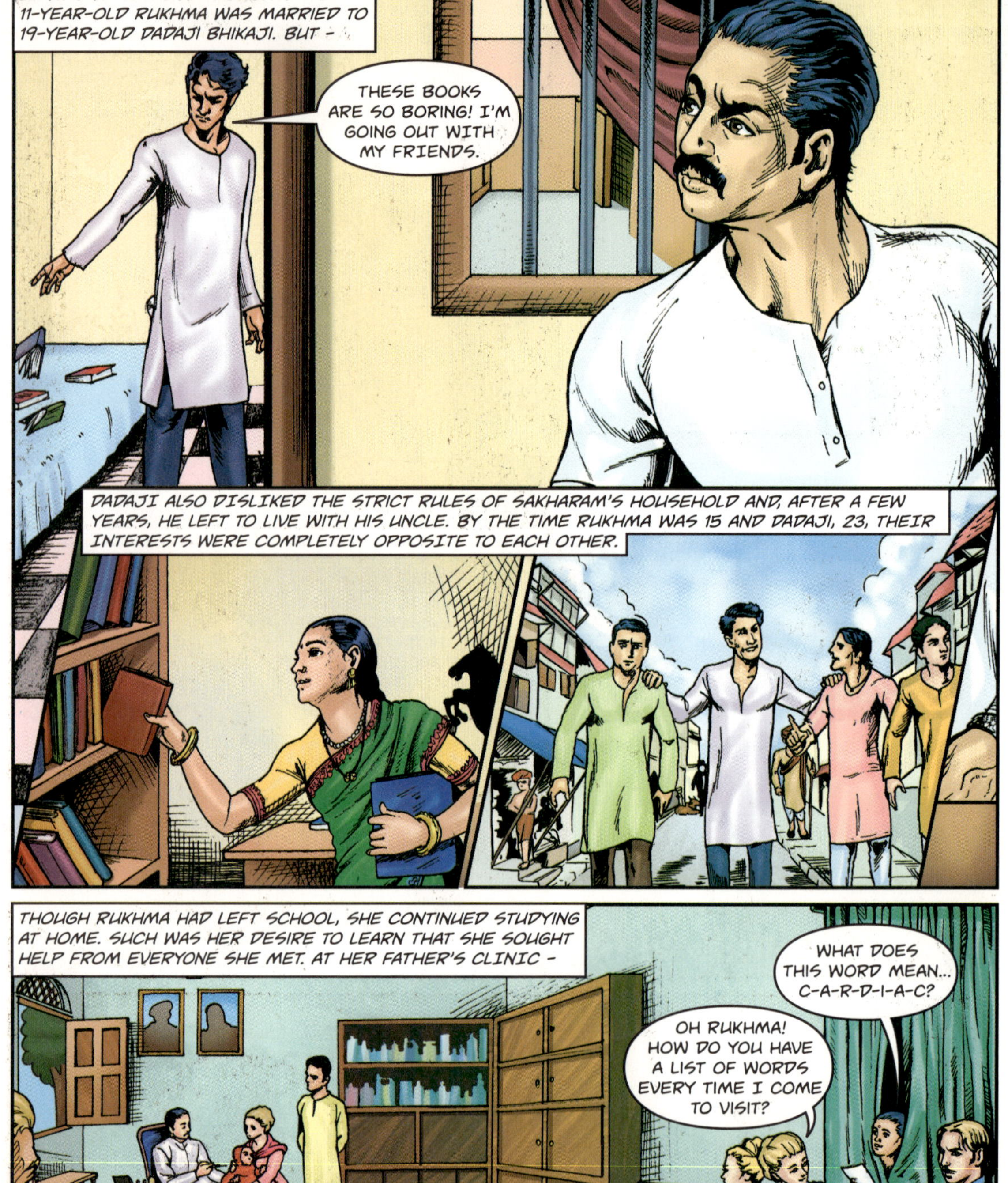
IT WAS WITH THESE THOUGHTS THAT 11-YEAR-OLD RUKHMA WAS MARRIED TO 19-YEAR-OLD DADAJI BHIKAJI. BUT -
THESE BOOKS ARE SO BORING! I'M GOING OUT WITH MY FRIENDS.
DADAJI ALSO DISLIKED THE STRICT RULES OF SAKHARAM'S HOUSEHOLD AND, AFTER A FEW YEARS, HE LEFT TO LIVE WITH HIS UNCLE. BY THE TIME RUKHMA WAS 15 AND DADAJI, 23, THEIR INTERESTS WERE COMPLETELY OPPOSITE TO EACH OTHER.
THOUGH RUKHMA HAD LEFT SCHOOL, SHE CONTINUED STUDYING AT HOME. SUCH WAS HER DESIRE TO LEARN THAT SHE SOUGHT HELP FROM EVERYONE SHE MET. AT HER FATHER'S CLINIC -
WHAT DOES THIS WORD MEAN... C-A-R-D-I-A-C?
OH RUKHMA! HOW DO YOU HAVE A LIST OF WORDS EVERY TIME I COME TO VISIT?

WHEN SHE WAS 19 -
YOU WILL SOON GO TO YOUR OWN HOUSE, RUKHMA. I WILL MISS YOU!
AAI, MY MIND IS SO FULL OF IDEAS. I WANT TO DO SOMETHING WITH MY LIFE.
OF COURSE YOU WILL! BEING A GOOD WIFE AND MOTHER IS THE MOST IMPORTANT THING A WOMAN CAN DO.
I WANT TO DO MORE THAN THAT, AAI. I WANT TO BECOME A DOCTOR.
A DOCTOR! ARE YOU OUT OF YOUR MIND!?
OW! WHY NOT? I WILL STUDY REALLY HARD. I KNOW I CAN BECOME ONE!
RUKHMA, YOU'RE MARRIED! YOU HAVE A HUSBAND! YOUR RESPONSIBILITY IS TO GO AND MAKE A LIFE WITH HIM.
I KNOW, BUT IF I BECOME A DOCTOR, I WILL BE ABLE TO HELP SO MANY WOMEN LIKE YOU AND ME. THINK OF THE CHANGE IT WILL BRING ABOUT.
IN THOSE DAYS, THERE WERE NO LADY DOCTORS. MOST WOMEN PREFERRED TO SUFFER IN SILENCE RATHER THAN GO TO A MALE DOCTOR.

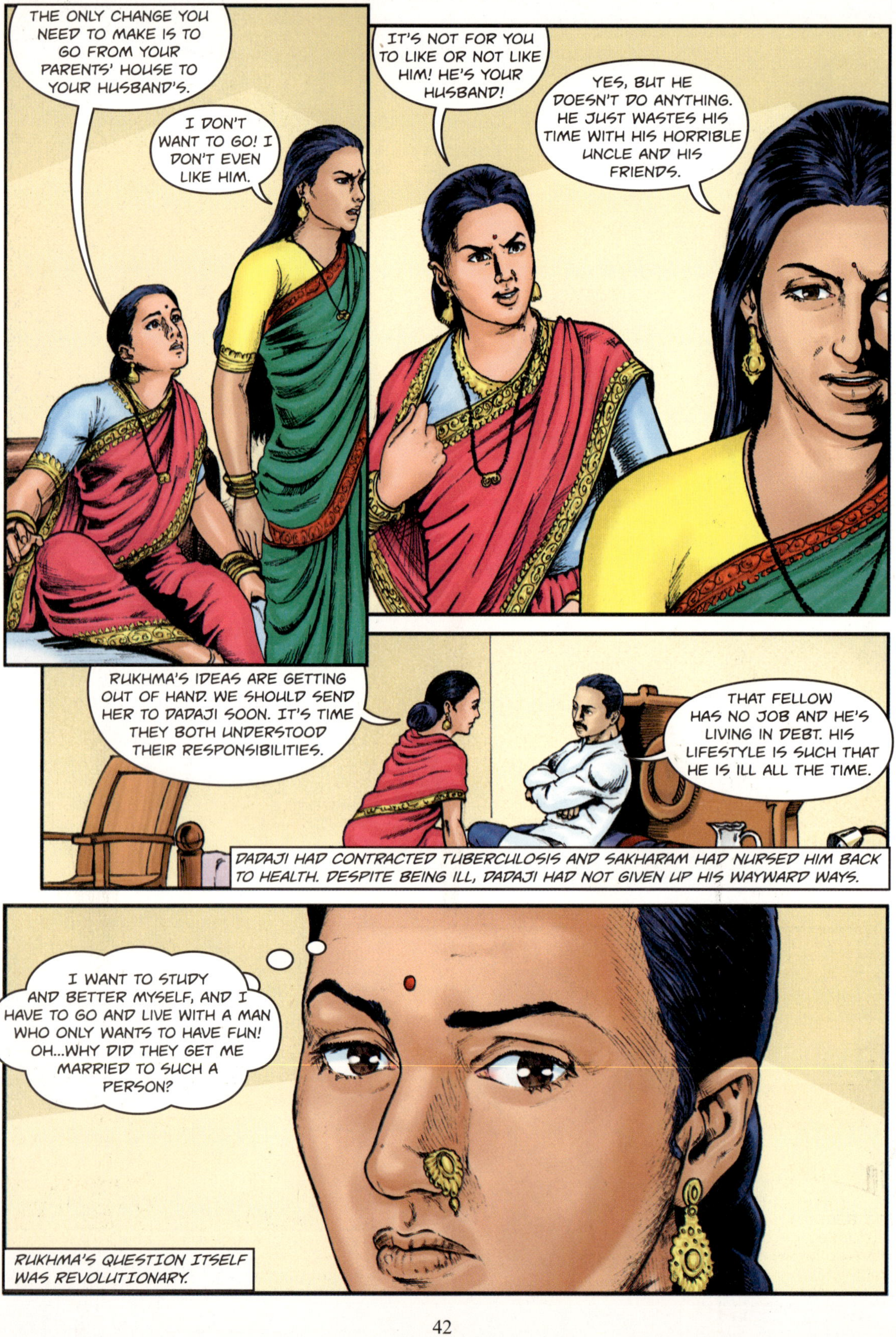

THE ONLY CHANGE YOU NEED TO MAKE IS TO GO FROM YOUR PARENTS' HOUSE TO YOUR HUSBAND'S.

I DON'T WANT TO GO! I DON'T EVEN LIKE HIM.

IT'S NOT FOR YOU TO LIKE OR NOT LIKE HIM! HE'S YOUR HUSBAND!

YES, BUT HE DOESN'T DO ANYTHING. HE JUST WASTES HIS TIME WITH HIS HORRIBLE UNCLE AND HIS FRIENDS.

RUKHMA'S IDEAS ARE GETTING OUT OF HAND. WE SHOULD SEND HER TO DADAJI SOON. IT'S TIME THEY BOTH UNDERSTOOD THEIR RESPONSIBILITIES.

THAT FELLOW HAS NO JOB AND HE'S LIVING IN DEBT. HIS LIFESTYLE IS SUCH THAT HE IS ILL ALL THE TIME.

DADAJI HAD CONTRACTED TUBERCULOSIS AND SAKHARAM HAD NURSED HIM BACK TO HEALTH. DESPITE BEING ILL, DADAJI HAD NOT GIVEN UP HIS WAYWARD WAYS.

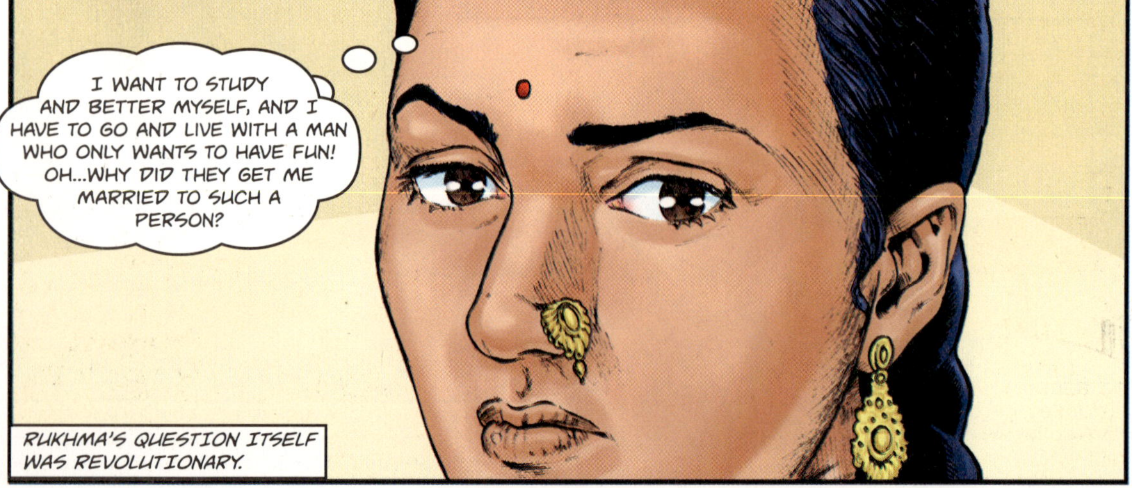

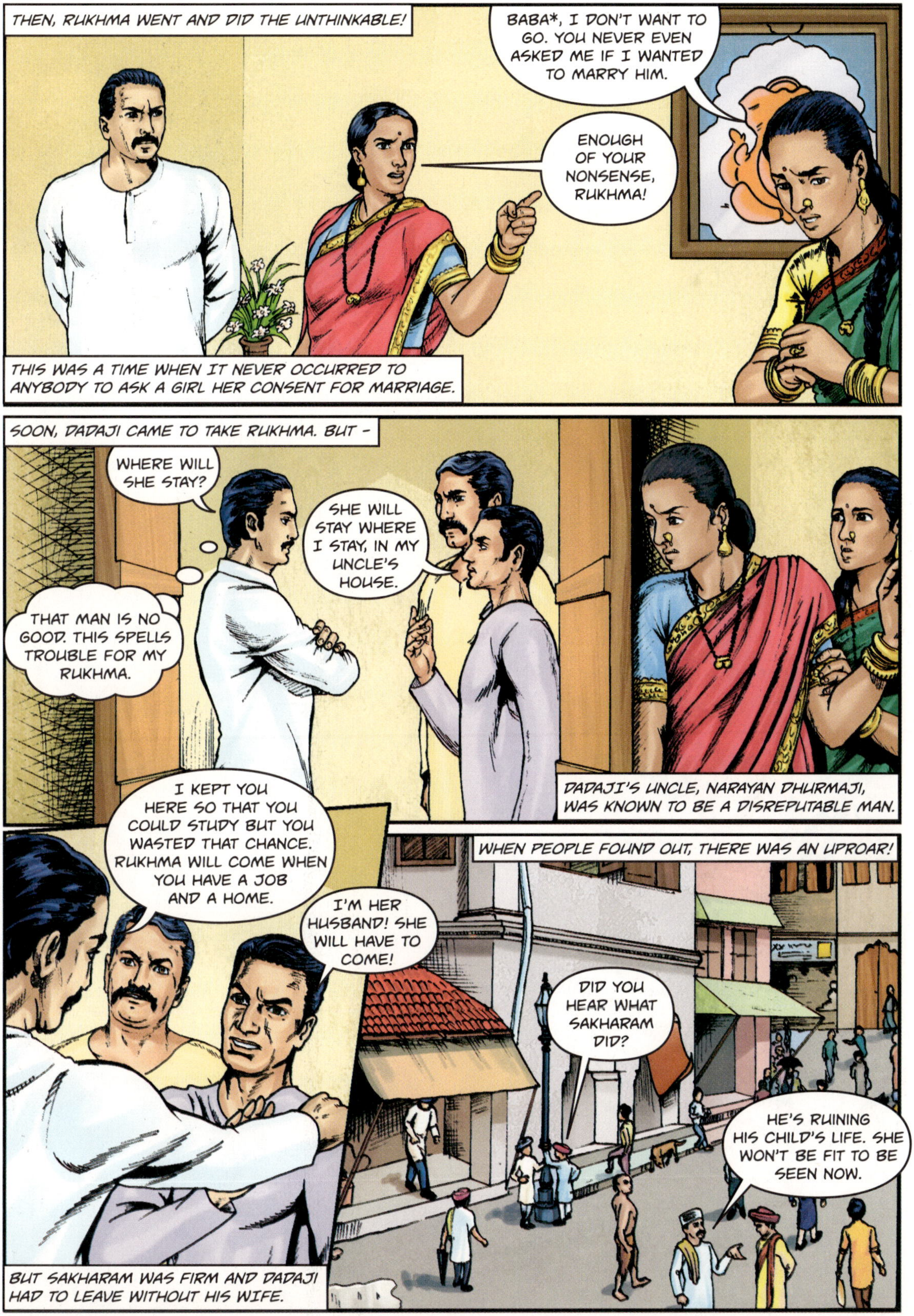

SOON, DADAJI CAME TO TAKE RUKHMA. BUT -

WHERE WILL SHE STAY?

SHE WILL STAY WHERE I STAY, IN MY UNCLE'S HOUSE.

THAT MAN IS NO GOOD. THIS SPELLS TROUBLE FOR MY RUKHMA.

DADAJI'S UNCLE, NARAYAN DHURMAJI, WAS KNOWN TO BE A DISREPUTABLE MAN.

I KEPT YOU HERE SO THAT YOU COULD STUDY BUT YOU WASTED THAT CHANCE. RUKHMA WILL COME WHEN YOU HAVE A JOB AND A HOME.

I'M HER HUSBAND! SHE WILL HAVE TO COME!

BUT SAKHARAM WAS FIRM AND DADAJI HAD TO LEAVE WITHOUT HIS WIFE.

WHEN PEOPLE FOUND OUT, THERE WAS AN UPROAR!

DID YOU HEAR WHAT SAKHARAM DID?

HE'S RUINING HIS CHILD'S LIFE. SHE WON'T BE FIT TO BE SEEN NOW.

*FATHER IN MARATHI

AT HOME –
HOW COULD HE DO THIS, BABA? A GIRL IS SUPPOSED TO GO WITH HER HUSBAND! WHERE WILL SHE GO NOW?
HE'S HER STEPFATHER...
...WHAT DOES HE CARE?
DADAJI, AT THE INSTIGATION OF HIS UNCLE, FILED A CASE AGAINST RUKHMA. ON 19 MARCH, 1884 –
LEGAL PAPERS? BUT DADAJI...I HAVE FED YOU, TAKEN CARE OF YOU....
RUKHMA BELONGS TO ME. SHE HAS NO CHOICE BUT TO COME HOME.
FOR RUKHMA, LIFE AS SHE KNEW IT WAS OVER. A LEGAL CASE WAS MOST DEFINITELY A FATE WORSE THAN DEATH.
The Times
ADAJI BHIKAJI
V/S RUKHMABAI
Child bride refuses to go home to husband!
NOT GOING TO HER HUSBAND! WHATEVER NEXT?
EVEN A WIDOW'S LIFE WILL BE BETTER THAN HERS. I WON'T ALLOW MY WIFE TO EVEN LOOK AT HER.

RUKHMA STARTED GETTING OSTRACISED AND HER FAMILY WAS DEVASTATED. BUT SHE FOUND THAT SHE WAS MADE OF STERNER STUFF.
LET THEM FIGHT A CASE! I NOW DESPISE DADAJI! WHY SHOULD I BE FORCED TO GO TO HIM? AM I NOT A PERSON? ARE WOMEN NOT PEOPLE TOO? WHY DO OUR FEELINGS NOT MATTER?
MARRIAGES ARE PLANNED ACCORDING TO EVERYONE ELSE'S CONVENIENCE. NOBODY EVEN THINKS ABOUT US...WE WHO HAVE TO LIVE THE LIFE THEY ARE IMPOSING ON US. WHY SHOULD WE NOT HAVE A SAY IN OUR OWN LIVES?
RUKHMA'S MOTHER AND MATERNAL GRANDFATHER WERE FURIOUS.
DADAJI IS YOUR SON-IN-LAW! YOU HAVE TO PLACATE HIM. HE MUST WITHDRAW THIS CASE.
ON THEIR INSISTENCE, SAKHARAM TRIED MAKING PEACE WITH DADAJI...
...BUT NOTHING WORKED. A FEW MONTHS LATER -
I HAVE TRIED EVERYTHING. HE REFUSES TO LISTEN.
AFTER EVERYTHING WE HAVE DONE FOR HIM! IT SEEMS HE JUST WANTS TO MAKE TROUBLE FOR US.

A FEW MONTHS LATER, IN APRIL, 1885, DR SAKHARAM SUDDENLY PASSED AWAY. RUKHMA FOUND HERSELF ALONE. THEN, HELP CAME FROM UNEXPECTED QUARTERS IN THE FORM OF THE RECENTLY PUBLISHED 'NOTES ON INFANT MARRIAGE AND ENFORCED WIDOWHOOD IN INDIA' BY SOCIAL REFORMER BEHRAMJI MALABARI.
SOMEBODY ELSE IS THINKING LIKE THIS? I'M NOT ALONE?
MALABARI HAD DETAILED THE PLIGHT OF CHILD BRIDES AND WIDOWS AND WAS ASKING THE BRITISH TO CHANGE THE LAW.
FOR RUKHMA, THE SITUATION HAD BECOME LESS ABOUT HERSELF AND MORE ABOUT THE PLIGHT OF WOMEN IN GENERAL.
I FEEL THAT FORTUNE IS ABOUT TO SMILE ON THE UNHAPPY DAUGHTERS OF INDIA.
MALABARI WAS ALSO THE EDITOR OF A NEWSPAPER, 'INDIAN SPECTATOR'. HE HAD PUBLISHED MANY ARTICLES ON THE NEED FOR SOCIAL REFORM.
RUKHMA'S CASE LED TO MANY DEBATES ACROSS THE COUNTRY. EVEN SOCIAL REFORMERS WERE DIVIDED IN THEIR OPINION. BUT ON 26 JUNE, 1885, A MOST UNUSUAL THING HAPPENED.
A LETTER FROM A HINDOO LADY? WHAT IS THAT?
I DON'T KNOW...BUT THERE IS A HUGE EDITORIAL INSISTING THAT WE READ IT.

THE TIMES OF INDIA HAD PUBLISHED A LETTER SIGNED 'A HINDOO LADY', SPEAKING ABOUT THE PLIGHT OF INDIAN WOMEN.
LETTERS TO THE EDITOR
In the prevailing customs, a woman cannot deny to live with her husband even on reasonable grounds. He may ill-treat her, beat her, drive her away, keep her without food, but she must submit to her lot and stay with him (if he keeps her with him)...
...We women have naturally come to look down upon ourselves but I wish to do something if in my power to ameliorate our present suffering. In the eyes of our lawmakers, men and women belong to quite different species of humanity....
SHE'S APPEALING FOR THE ADDITION OF JUST ONE SENTENCE - THAT THE LEGAL AGE FOR MARRIAGE BE INCREASED TO 20 FOR BOYS AND 15 FOR GIRLS.
SUCH A SPIRITED LETTER! WHO IS SHE?
INDIA WAS AGOG! NEVER BEFORE HAD AN INDIAN WOMAN ASSERTED ANY RIGHT TO HERSELF OR PERCEIVED HERSELF AS AN INDIVIDUAL. THOUGH NO ONE KNEW THAT THE HINDOO LADY WAS RUKHMA, THE CONTENTS OF THE LETTER SHONE A NEW LIGHT ON THE DADAJI BHIKAJI V/S RUKHMABAI CASE.

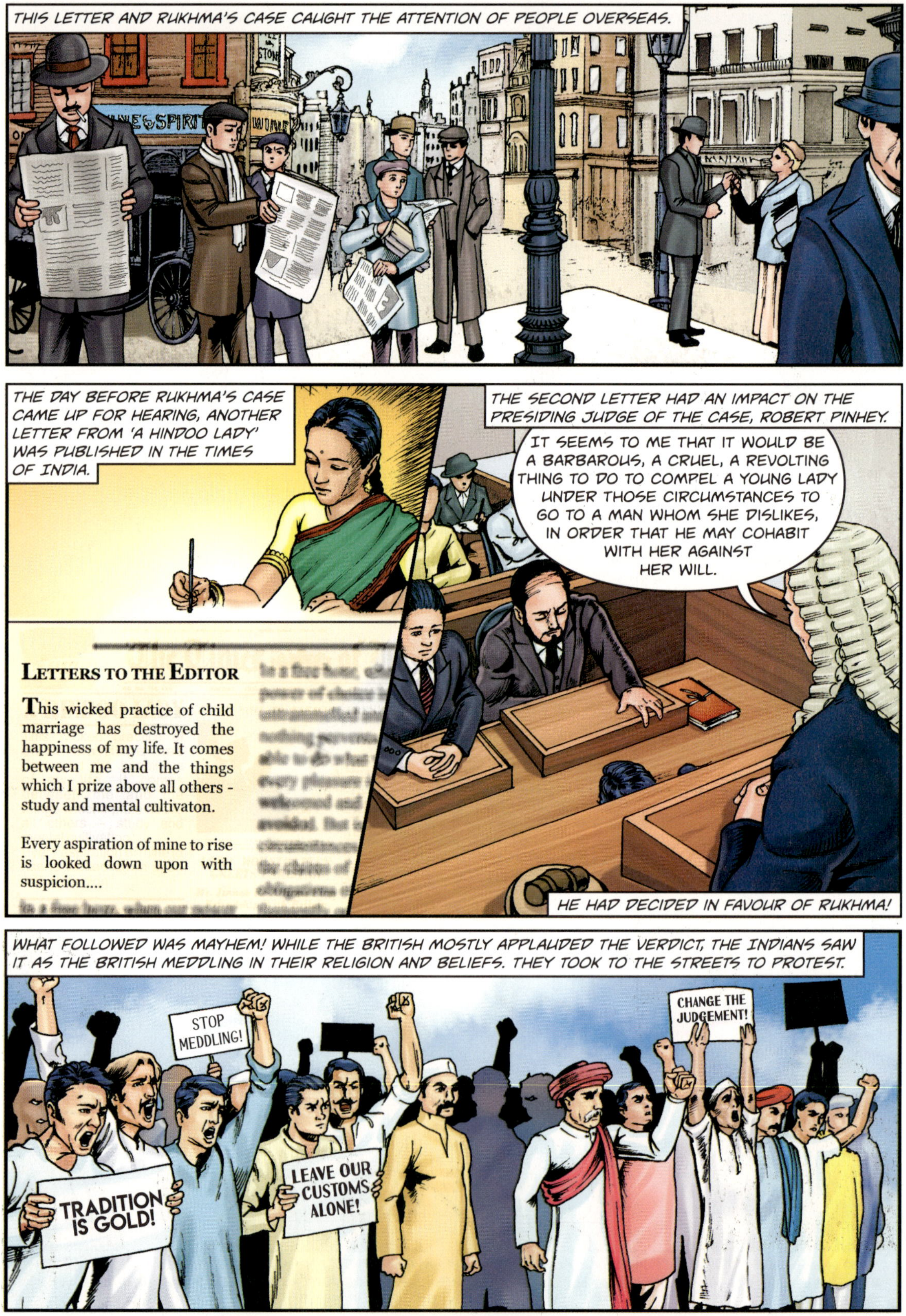

THE DAY BEFORE RUKHMA'S CASE CAME UP FOR HEARING, ANOTHER LETTER FROM 'A HINDOO LADY' WAS PUBLISHED IN THE TIMES OF INDIA.

LETTERS TO THE EDITOR

This wicked practice of child marriage has destroyed the happiness of my life. It comes between me and the things which I prize above all others - study and mental cultivaton.

Every aspiration of mine to rise is looked down upon with suspicion....

THE SECOND LETTER HAD AN IMPACT ON THE PRESIDING JUDGE OF THE CASE, ROBERT PINHEY.

IT SEEMS TO ME THAT IT WOULD BE A BARBAROUS, A CRUEL, A REVOLTING THING TO DO TO COMPEL A YOUNG LADY UNDER THOSE CIRCUMSTANCES TO GO TO A MAN WHOM SHE DISLIKES, IN ORDER THAT HE MAY COHABIT WITH HER AGAINST HER WILL.

HE HAD DECIDED IN FAVOUR OF RUKHMA!

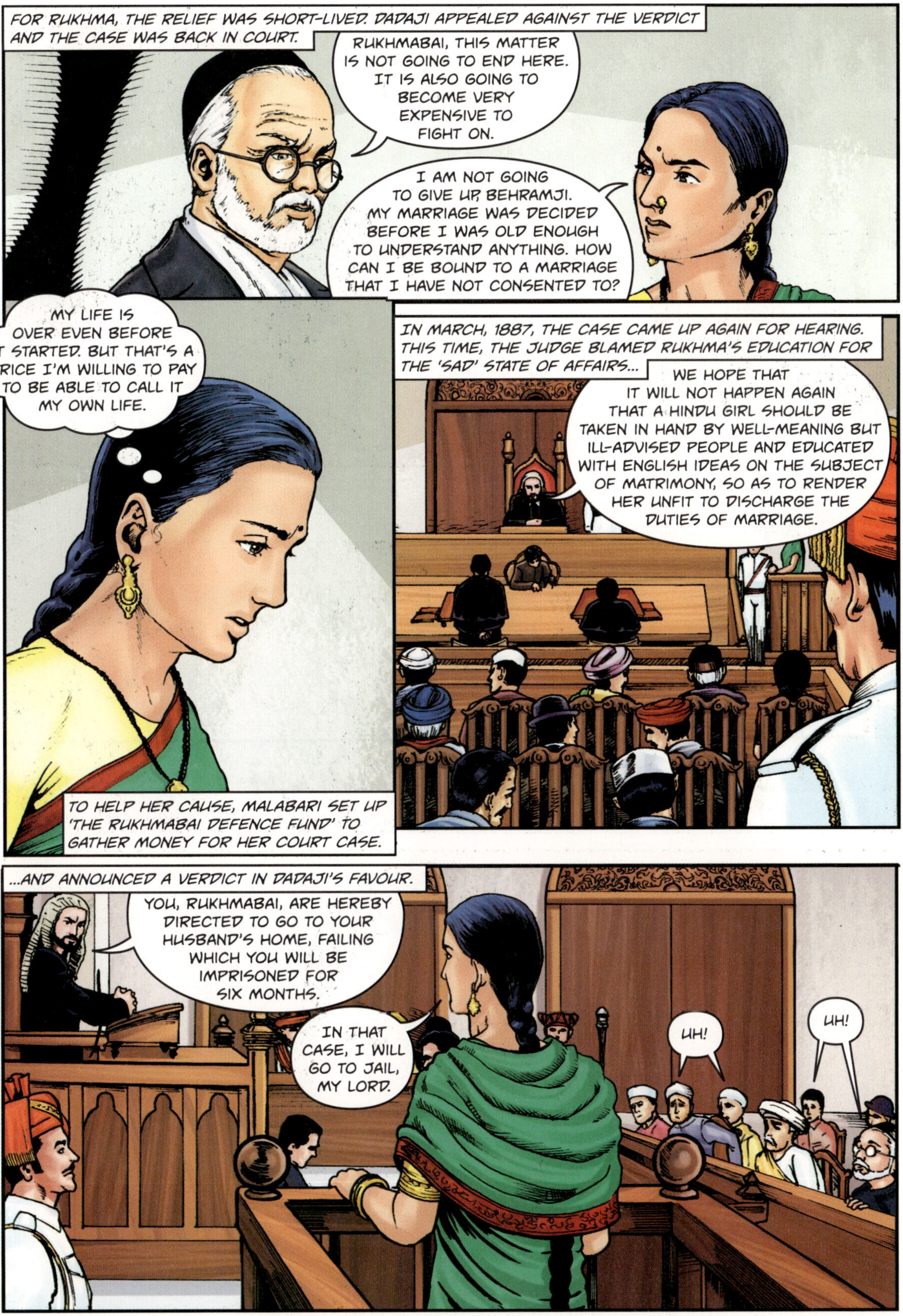

FOR RUKHMA, THE RELIEF WAS SHORT-LIVED. DADAJI APPEALED AGAINST THE VERDICT AND THE CASE WAS BACK IN COURT.

RUKHMABAI, THIS MATTER IS NOT GOING TO END HERE. IT IS ALSO GOING TO BECOME VERY EXPENSIVE TO FIGHT ON.

I AM NOT GOING TO GIVE UP, BEHRAMJI. MY MARRIAGE WAS DECIDED BEFORE I WAS OLD ENOUGH TO UNDERSTAND ANYTHING. HOW CAN I BE BOUND TO A MARRIAGE THAT I HAVE NOT CONSENTED TO?

MY LIFE IS OVER EVEN BEFORE IT STARTED. BUT THAT'S A PRICE I'M WILLING TO PAY TO BE ABLE TO CALL IT MY OWN LIFE.

TO HELP HER CAUSE, MALABARI SET UP 'THE RUKHMABAI DEFENCE FUND' TO GATHER MONEY FOR HER COURT CASE.

IN MARCH, 1887, THE CASE CAME UP AGAIN FOR HEARING. THIS TIME, THE JUDGE BLAMED RUKHMA'S EDUCATION FOR THE 'SAD' STATE OF AFFAIRS...

WE HOPE THAT IT WILL NOT HAPPEN AGAIN THAT A HINDU GIRL SHOULD BE TAKEN IN HAND BY WELL-MEANING BUT ILL-ADVISED PEOPLE AND EDUCATED WITH ENGLISH IDEAS ON THE SUBJECT OF MATRIMONY, SO AS TO RENDER HER UNFIT TO DISCHARGE THE DUTIES OF MARRIAGE.

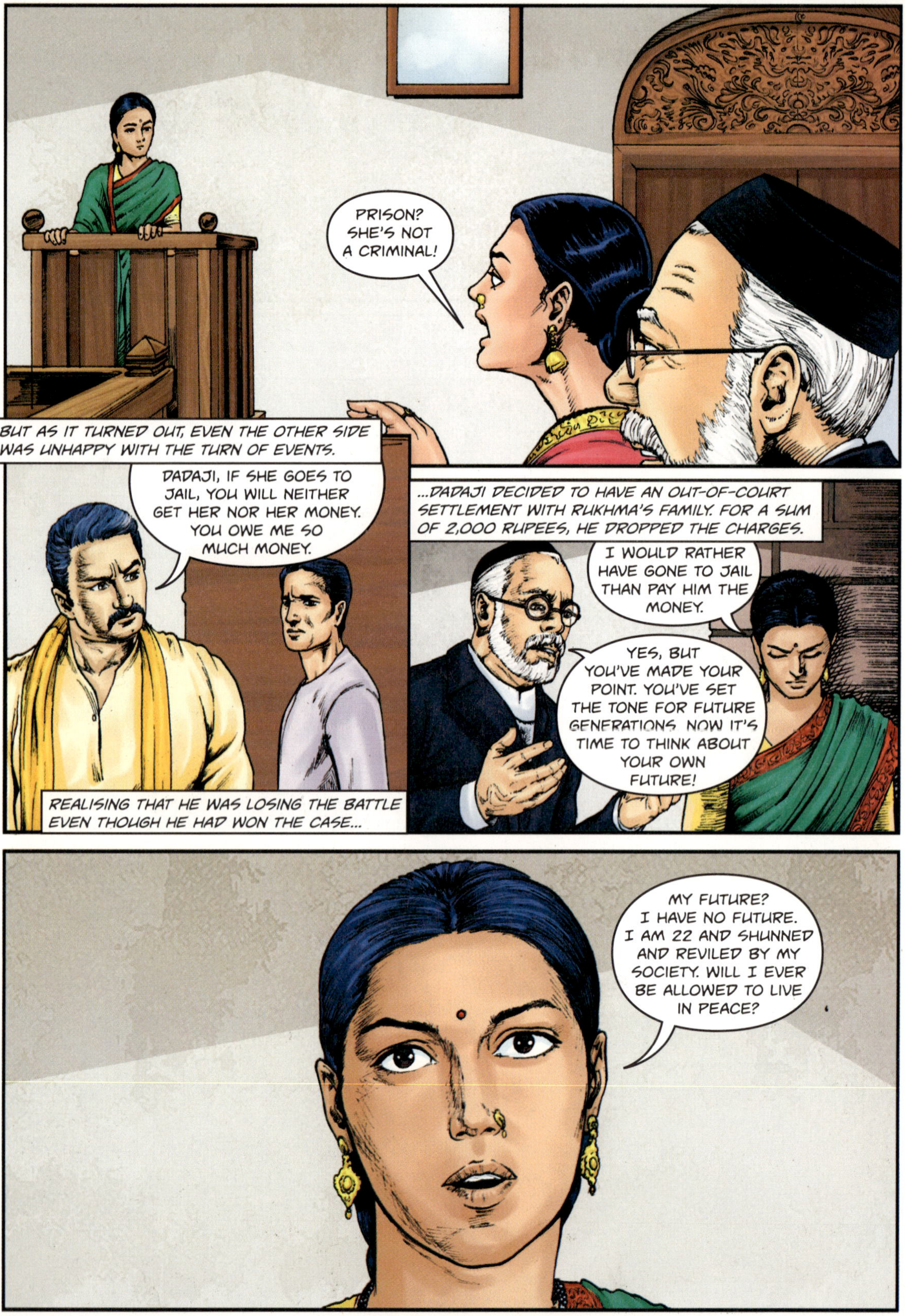

PRISON? SHE'S NOT A CRIMINAL!

BUT AS IT TURNED OUT, EVEN THE OTHER SIDE WAS UNHAPPY WITH THE TURN OF EVENTS.

DADAJI, IF SHE GOES TO JAIL, YOU WILL NEITHER GET HER NOR HER MONEY. YOU OWE ME SO MUCH MONEY.

REALISING THAT HE WAS LOSING THE BATTLE EVEN THOUGH HE HAD WON THE CASE...

...DADAJI DECIDED TO HAVE AN OUT-OF-COURT SETTLEMENT WITH RUKHMA'S FAMILY. FOR A SUM OF 2,000 RUPEES, HE DROPPED THE CHARGES.

I WOULD RATHER HAVE GONE TO JAIL THAN PAY HIM THE MONEY.

YES, BUT YOU'VE MADE YOUR POINT. YOU'VE SET THE TONE FOR FUTURE GENERATIONS. NOW IT'S TIME TO THINK ABOUT YOUR OWN FUTURE!

RUKHMA'S LIFE WAS TO CHANGE DIRECTION YET AGAIN!
RUKHMABAI, I KNOW THAT WHEN YOU WERE YOUNGER, YOU WANTED TO BECOME A DOCTOR. DO YOU STILL WANT TO BECOME ONE?
THE LADY WAS EDITH PECHEY-PHIPSON, ONE OF ENGLAND'S FIRST WOMEN DOCTORS WHO WAS WORKING IN BOMBAY'S CAMA HOSPITAL.
YOU HAVE A LOVE FOR KNOWLEDGE AND A COURAGE THAT WILL SERVE YOU AND YOUR WOMENFOLK WELL. IF YOU AGREE, I CAN TRY AND ARRANGE FOR FUNDS FOR YOUR EDUCATION.
RUKHMA COULD NOT BELIEVE HER EARS! SHE WAS FINALLY HEARING SOMETHING GOOD. SHE IMMEDIATELY AGREED AND TOOK A COURSE TO LEARN ENGLISH.

THEN, IN 1888, RUKHMABAI SET SAIL FOR ENGLAND.
AM I REALLY ON THE THRESHOLD OF ACHIEVING MY DREAM?

IN ENGLAND, RUKHMA STUDIED AT THE LONDON SCHOOL OF MEDICINE FOR WOMEN. EVERYTHING WAS STRANGE AND SHE WAS ALONE. IT WAS TOUGH BUT SHE WAS TOUGHER.

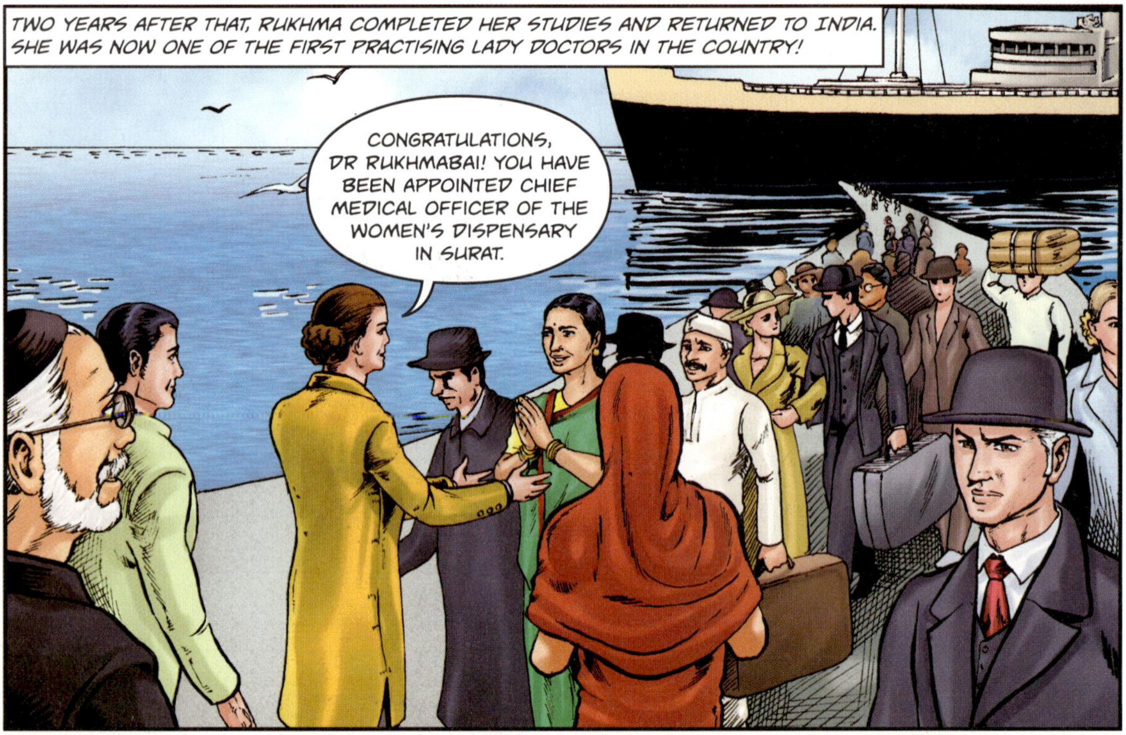

TWO YEARS AFTER THAT, RUKHMA COMPLETED HER STUDIES AND RETURNED TO INDIA. SHE WAS NOW ONE OF THE FIRST PRACTISING LADY DOCTORS IN THE COUNTRY!

CONGRATULATIONS, DR RUKHMABAI! YOU HAVE BEEN APPOINTED CHIEF MEDICAL OFFICER OF THE WOMEN'S DISPENSARY IN SURAT.

HER STRUGGLES, HOWEVER, WERE FAR FROM OVER. SHE WAS OSTRACISED EVEN IN SURAT.

IT'S BEEN THREE DAYS! WHY IS NO ONE COMING TO THE HOSPITAL?

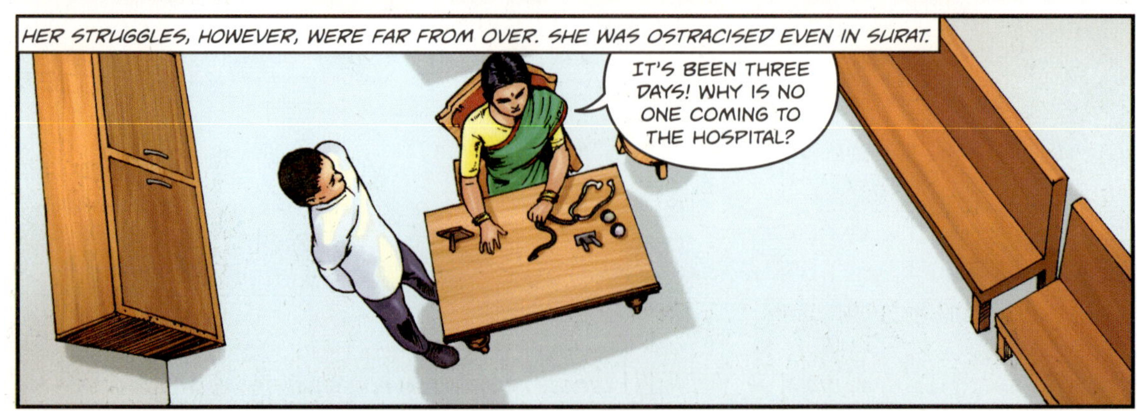

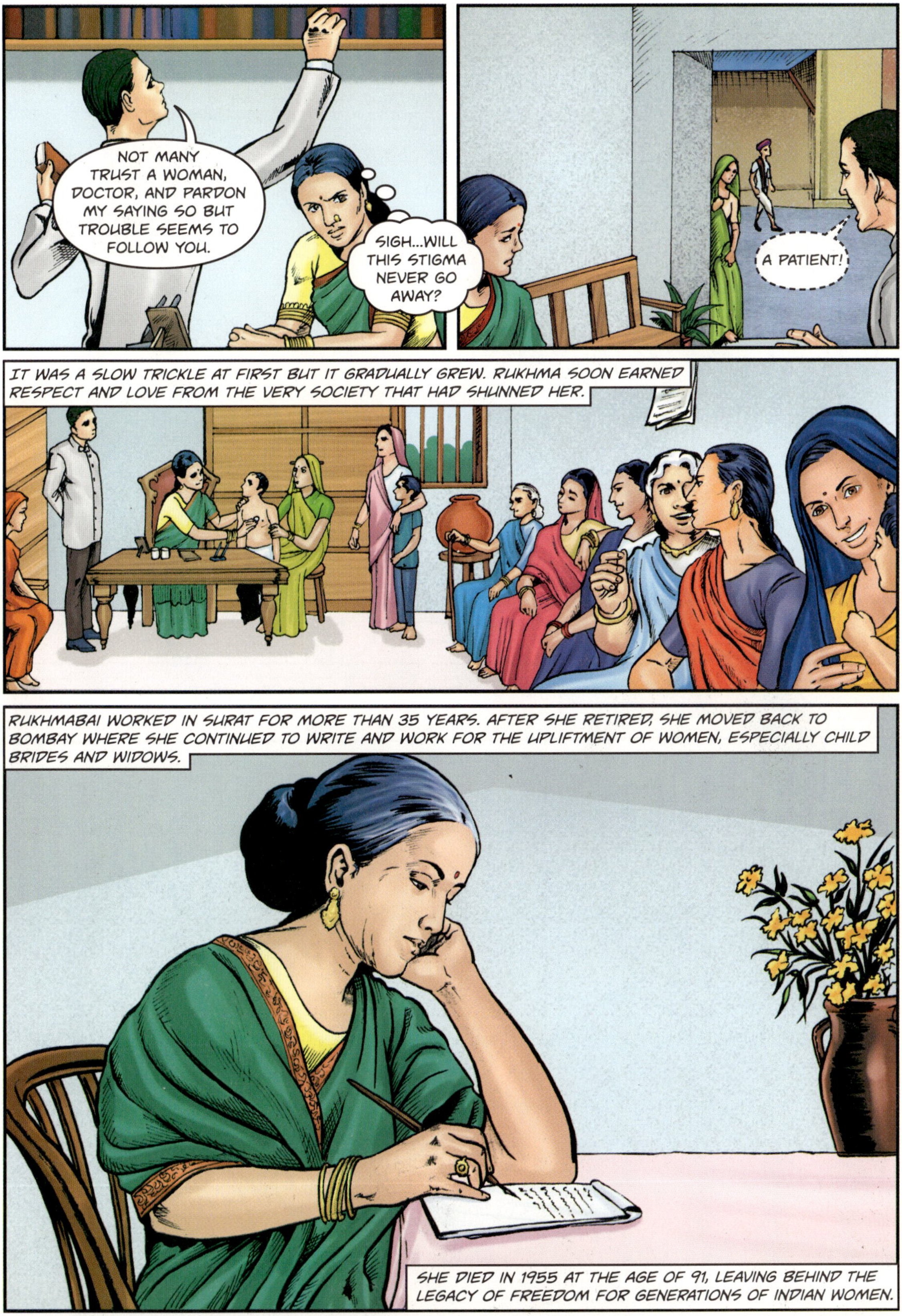

RUKHMABAI WORKED IN SURAT FOR MORE THAN 35 YEARS. AFTER SHE RETIRED, SHE MOVED BACK TO BOMBAY WHERE SHE CONTINUED TO WRITE AND WORK FOR THE UPLIFTMENT OF WOMEN, ESPECIALLY CHILD BRIDES AND WIDOWS.

SHE DIED IN 1955 AT THE AGE OF 91, LEAVING BEHIND THE LEGACY OF FREEDOM FOR GENERATIONS OF INDIAN WOMEN.

Muthulakshmi Reddy - First woman legislator

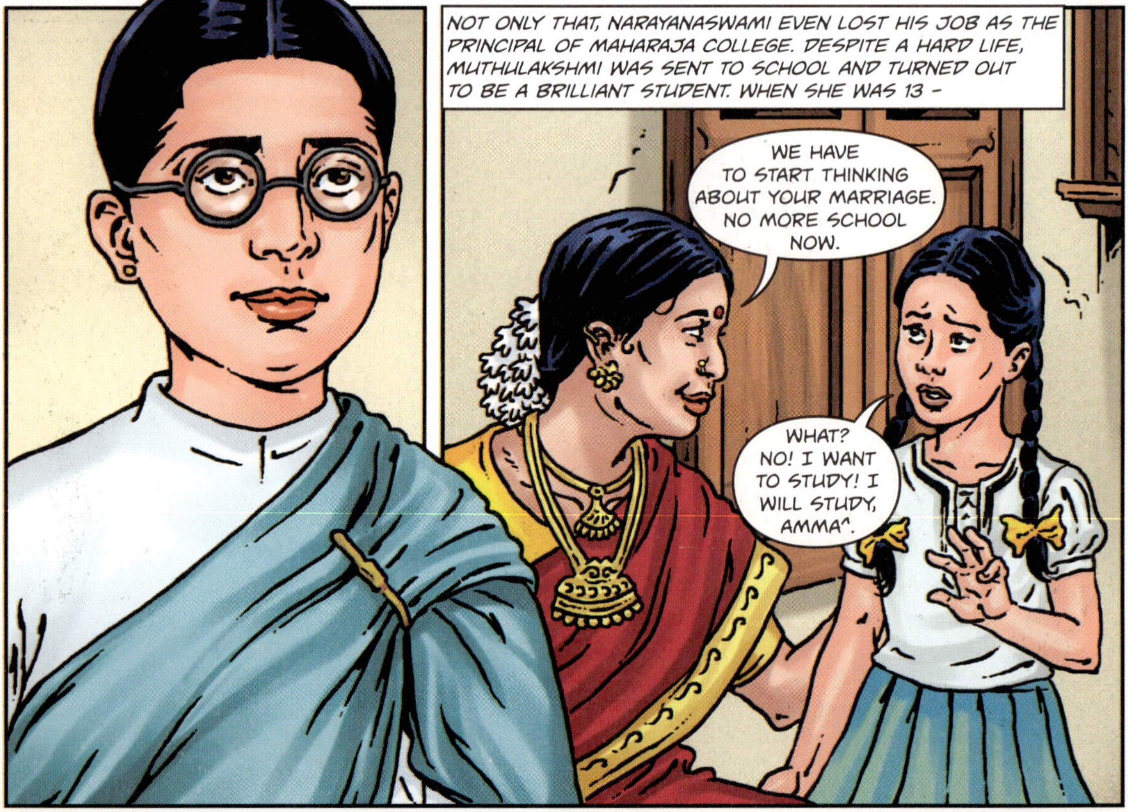

MUTHULAKSHMI WAS BORN ON 30 JULY, 1886, IN THE PRINCELY STATE OF PUDUKKOTTAI, WHICH IS NOW A PART OF TAMIL NADU. THE ELDEST DAUGHTER OF NARAYANASWAMI IYER AND CHANDRAMMAL, HER PARENTS HAD ALREADY CAUSED A SCANDAL WHEN THEY HAD DECIDED TO GET MARRIED.

NOT ONLY THAT, NARAYANASWAMI EVEN LOST HIS JOB AS THE PRINCIPAL OF MAHARAJA COLLEGE. DESPITE A HARD LIFE, MUTHULAKSHMI WAS SENT TO SCHOOL AND TURNED OUT TO BE A BRILLIANT STUDENT. WHEN SHE WAS 13 –

WE HAVE TO START THINKING ABOUT YOUR MARRIAGE. NO MORE SCHOOL NOW.

WHAT? NO! I WANT TO STUDY! I WILL STUDY, AMMA^.

*THERE WAS A PREVAILING CUSTOM IN WHICH YOUNG GIRLS WERE DEDICATED AS 'DEVADASIS' OR WOMEN WHO WERE MARRIED TO GOD.

^MOTHER IN TAMIL

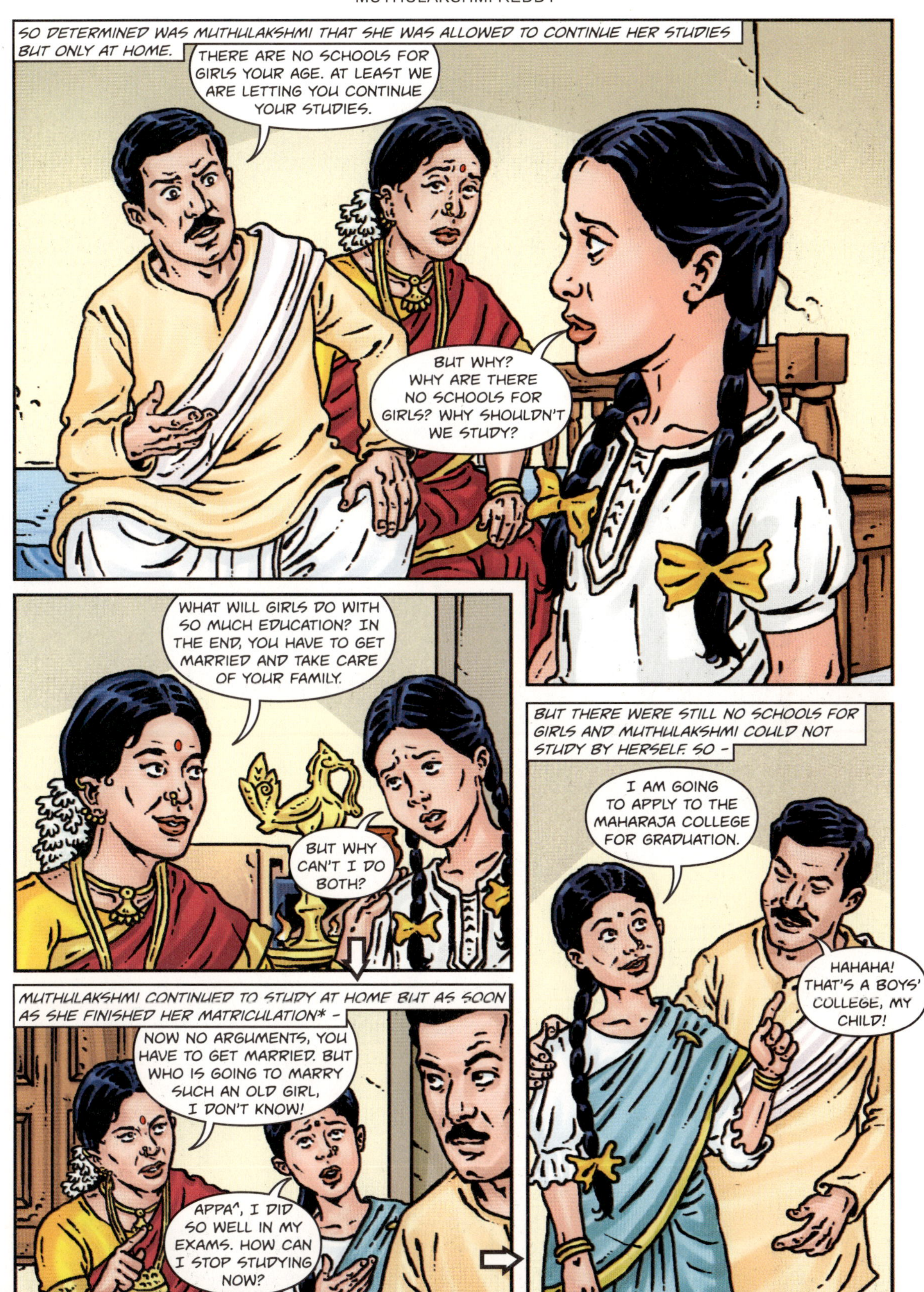

*CLASS 10
^FATHER IN TAMIL

DOESN'T MATTER, I WILL STUDY THERE!
SHE WENT AHEAD AND APPLIED FOR ADMISSION.
MUTHULAKSHMI WAS NOT ONE TO ACCEPT DEFEAT. SHE WROTE TO THE MAHARAJA OF PUDUKKOTTAI TELLING HIM OF HER PLIGHT.
HMMM... WHAT A BRIGHT AND SPIRITED CHILD!
INITIALLY EVERYONE LAUGHED BUT WHEN THEY SAW THAT SHE WAS SERIOUS, THE PRINCIPAL SUMMONED MUTHULAKSHMI AND HER FATHER.
CONTROL YOUR DAUGHTER, MR NARAYANASWAMI. DOES SHE KNOW WHAT SHE'S DOING?
ENOUGH OF THIS NONSENSE, MUTHU! I SHOULDN'T HAVE LET YOU STUDY SO MUCH. YOU'VE LOST YOUR MIND.
THE MAHARAJA GRANTED HER ADMISSION AND A SCHOLARSHIP. MUTHULAKSHMI'S PARENTS COULD NOT REFUSE BUT THE REST OF PUDUKKOTTAI WAS UP IN ARMS.
PRINCIPA
WE'RE TAKING OUR SONS OUT OF THIS COLLEGE. SHE WILL CORRUPT THEM!
I MYSELF DON'T WANT HER HERE BUT HOW CAN I GO AGAINST THE MAHARAJA'S WISHES?

AND EVERY TIME MUTHULAKSHMI STEPPED OUT OF HER HOME TO GO TO COLLEGE...
SPLAT
BANG
SPLOTCH
...MOBS PELTED HER WITH SLIPPERS! BUT SHE DID NOT LET ANYTHING STOP HER AND BECAME ONE AMONG THE HANDFUL OF WOMEN GRADUATES IN THE COUNTRY. SHE WAS ALSO THE FIRST WOMAN IN INDIA TO GO TO A BOYS' COLLEGE!

BY NOW, HER PARENTS HAD REALISED THAT THEIR DAUGHTER WAS DIFFERENT AND DID NOT TRY TO STOP HER. MUTHULAKSHMI USED THIS HARD-WON FREEDOM TO GO TO MADRAS AND STUDY MEDICINE.
MY COUSIN DIED WHILE GIVING BIRTH. I WANT TO TRY AND SAVE OTHER WOMEN FROM SUCH A FATE.
IT'S A TOUGH COURSE AND YOU WILL BE ALL ALONE. ARE YOU SURE?

SHE WAS SURE. NOT JUST THAT, SHE WAS BRILLIANT! AT HER GRADUATION IN 1912 -
FOR THE FIRST TIME IN THE HISTORY OF MADRAS MEDICAL COLLEGE, A WOMAN HAS STUDIED MEDICINE. MUTHULAKSHMI HAS SUCCESSFULLY COMPLETED HER COURSE BUT MORE THAN THAT...

...SHE HAS STOOD FIRST, A GOLD MEDALLIST IN MEDICINE!
CLAP!
CLAP!
CLAP!
CLAP!

*FREEDOM FIGHTER AND POET WHO BELIEVED IN WOMEN'S LIBERATION

^SUPPORTER OF INDIAN INDEPENDENCE, WRITER AND WOMEN'S RIGHTS ACTIVIST

**EDUCATIONIST, WOMEN'S RIGHTS ACTIVIST WHO WROTE THE MUSIC FOR THE INDIAN NATIONAL ANTHEM

*FELLOWSHIP OF THE ROYAL COLLEGES OF SURGEONS

IN 1916, ANNIE BESANT LAUNCHED THE 'HOME RULE' MOVEMENT. MUTHULAKSHMI SOON BECAME A PART OF THE CORE GROUP.

REAL FREEDOM FOR WOMEN WILL ONLY COME WHEN WE HAVE LAWS THAT SUPPORT US.

THE LAWS ARE ALL MADE BY MEN, SO THEY SUPPORT MEN!

WOMEN SHOULD ALSO BE ABLE TO MAKE LAWS.

WE CAN'T EVEN VOTE, FORGET ABOUT MAKING LAWS.

YES, WOMEN SHOULD BE ALLOWED TO VOTE. WE SHOULD HAVE A SAY IN THE GOVERNMENT.

SUCH THOUGHTS AND DISCUSSIONS LED THEM TO FORM THE 'WOMEN'S INDIAN ASSOCIATION' (WIA)* IN 1917. THEIR AIM WAS TO INSPIRE WOMEN TO BE MORE ACTIVE IN SOCIETY.

EQUALITY SHOULD BE BOTH SOCIAL AND POLITICAL.

THE WIA SOON BECAME AN IMPORTANT ORGANISATION. IT BROUGHT WOMEN TOGETHER FOR SELF-DEVELOPMENT AND THE SERVICE OF OTHERS. LATER, MUTHULAKSHMI WOULD BE ITS PRESIDENT FOR MANY YEARS.

THEY SOON REALISED THAT WOMEN ALL OVER THE WORLD WERE STRUGGLING TO BE HEARD.

WE AREN'T ALONE IN OUR FIGHT. WOMEN IN ENGLAND AND IRELAND ARE ALSO FIGHTING FOR THEIR RIGHT TO VOTE.

I WISH THERE WAS A WAY WE COULD COMMUNICATE OUR THOUGHTS WITH EACH OTHER.

*THE WOMEN'S INDIAN ASSOCIATION (WIA) EXISTS EVEN TODAY. IT CELEBRATED ITS CENTENARY IN 2017.

*SECRETARY OF STATE FOR INDIA
^NOW CHENNAI

**THESE WERE LIMITED VOTING RIGHTS, NOT THE UNIVERSAL FRANCHISE THAT WE ALL ENJOY TODAY.

HOW WILL I DO IT? WILL I HAVE TIME FOR MY MEDICAL PRACTICE?
YOU WILL BE ABLE TO HELP A LOT MORE WOMEN THIS WAY.
SO, IN 1926, MUTHULAKSHMI BECAME THE FIRST-EVER WOMAN LEGISLATOR OF INDIA!
ALL WOMEN MANAGE THEIR HOUSEHOLDS. WE JUST NEED TO REALISE THAT OUR COUNTRY IS LIKE OUR LARGER FAMILY AND THAT WE CAN CONTRIBUTE TOWARDS ITS WELL-BEING.
IN JANUARY, 1927, SHE WAS ELECTED AS THE DEPUTY PRESIDENT OF THE COUNCIL. SHE WAS THE FIRST WOMAN IN THE WORLD TO EVER REACH SUCH A POSITION!
MY ELEVATION TO THIS POST IS AN HONOUR TO ALL INDIAN WOMEN. YOU HAVE DEMONSTRATED TO THE WORLD THAT YOU HAVE RIGHTLY UNDERSTOOD THE POWER AND INFLUENCE OF WOMEN, NOT ONLY IN THE INNER LIFE OF YOUR HOMES BUT ALSO IN THE WIDER SPHERE OF YOUR PUBLIC ACTIVITIES.
SHE SOON FIGURED OUT HOW THINGS WORKED AND STARTED MAKING HER MARK.
EDUCATION AND HEALTH FACILITIES FOR WOMEN AND CHILDREN?
YES, THERE IS A DIRE NEED FOR THOSE.

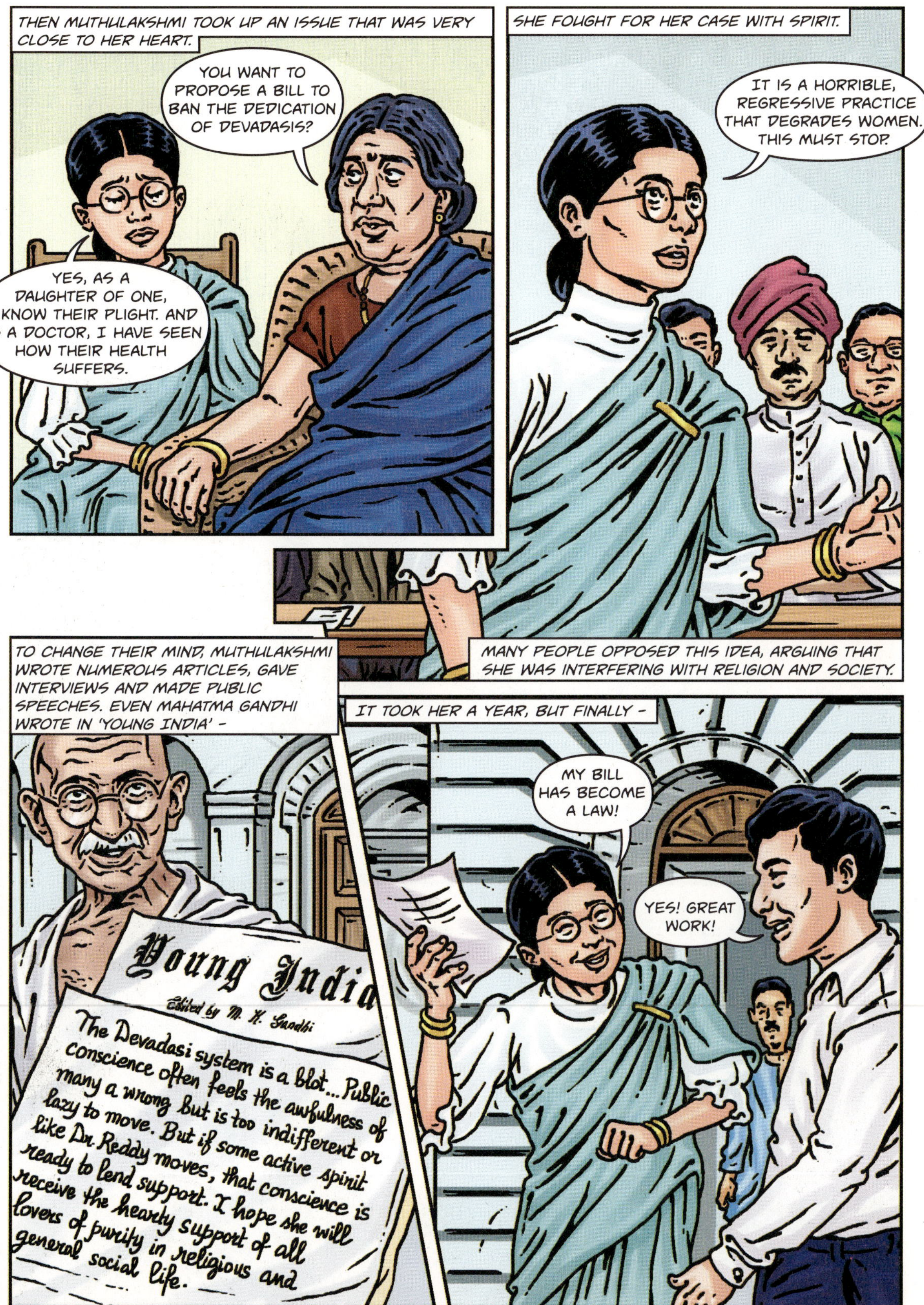
THEN MUTHULAKSHMI TOOK UP AN ISSUE THAT WAS VERY CLOSE TO HER HEART.
YOU WANT TO PROPOSE A BILL TO BAN THE DEDICATION OF DEVADASIS?
YES, AS A DAUGHTER OF ONE, KNOW THEIR PLIGHT. AND S A DOCTOR, I HAVE SEEN HOW THEIR HEALTH SUFFERS.
SHE FOUGHT FOR HER CASE WITH SPIRIT.
IT IS A HORRIBLE, REGRESSIVE PRACTICE THAT DEGRADES WOMEN. THIS MUST STOP.
MANY PEOPLE OPPOSED THIS IDEA, ARGUING THAT SHE WAS INTERFERING WITH RELIGION AND SOCIETY.
TO CHANGE THEIR MIND, MUTHULAKSHMI WROTE NUMEROUS ARTICLES, GAVE INTERVIEWS AND MADE PUBLIC SPEECHES. EVEN MAHATMA GANDHI WROTE IN 'YOUNG INDIA' –
Young India
Edited by M. K. Gandhi
The Devadasi system is a blot... Public conscience often feels the awfulness of many a wrong but is too indifferent or lazy to move. But if some active spirit like Dr. Reddy moves, that conscience is ready to lend support. I hope she will receive the hearty support of all lovers of purity in religious and general social life.
IT TOOK HER A YEAR, BUT FINALLY –
MY BILL HAS BECOME A LAW!
YES! GREAT WORK!

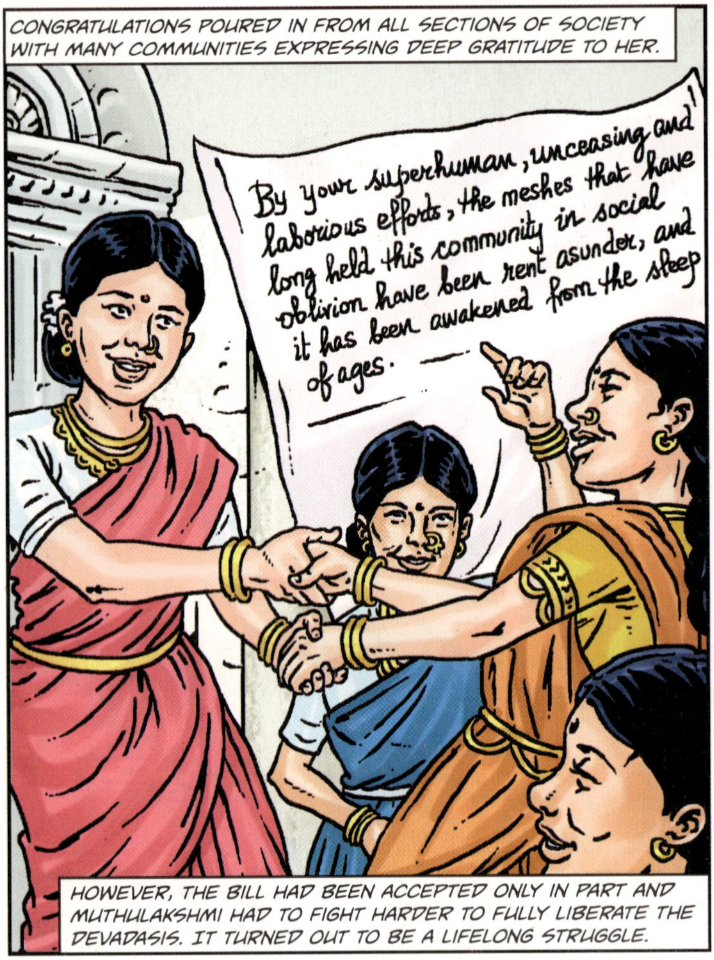

CONGRATULATIONS POURED IN FROM ALL SECTIONS OF SOCIETY WITH MANY COMMUNITIES EXPRESSING DEEP GRATITUDE TO HER.

By your superhuman, unceasing and laborious efforts, the meshes that have long held this community in social oblivion have been rent asunder, and it has been awakened from the sleep of ages.

HOWEVER, THE BILL HAD BEEN ACCEPTED ONLY IN PART AND MUTHULAKSHMI HAD TO FIGHT HARDER TO FULLY LIBERATE THE DEVADASIS. IT TURNED OUT TO BE A LIFELONG STRUGGLE.

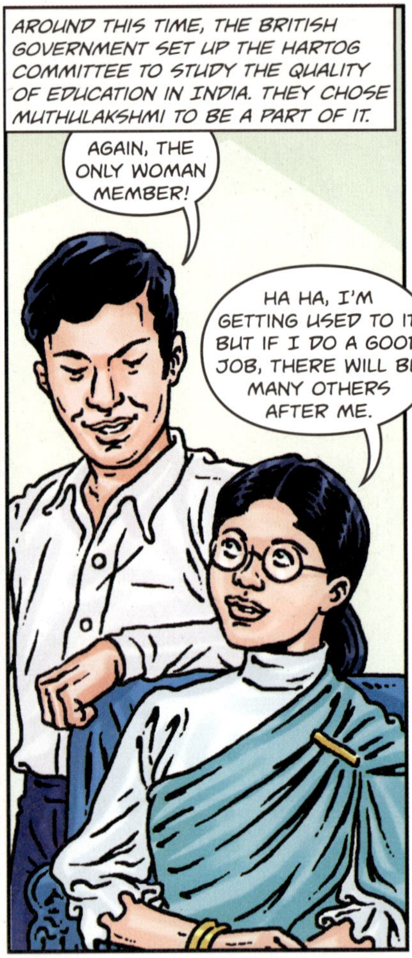

AROUND THIS TIME, THE BRITISH GOVERNMENT SET UP THE HARTOG COMMITTEE TO STUDY THE QUALITY OF EDUCATION IN INDIA. THEY CHOSE MUTHULAKSHMI TO BE A PART OF IT.

AGAIN, THE ONLY WOMAN MEMBER!

HA HA, I'M GETTING USED TO IT. BUT IF I DO A GOOD JOB, THERE WILL BE MANY OTHERS AFTER ME.

BY NOW, MUTHULAKSHMI HAD ALSO BECOME A FREEDOM FIGHTER AND A FOLLOWER OF MAHATMA GANDHI.
GANDHIJI TELLS US ABOUT NON-VIOLENCE. WHO CAN UNDERSTAND THAT BETTER THAN US, THE WOMEN OF INDIA? WE MUST CARRY HIS MESSAGE FORWARD.
IN 1930, WHEN GANDHIJI WAS ARRESTED FOLLOWING THE DANDI MARCH, MUTHULAKSHMI WAS SO SHOCKED THAT SHE RESIGNED FROM THE MADRAS LEGISLATURE IN PROTEST.

BUT SHE CONTINUED HER REFORM WORK WITH THE WIA. SHE WAS NOW EDITING STRI DHARMA AND THROUGH IT, WAS ABLE TO CARRY ON HER FIGHT FOR NATIONALISM AND WOMEN'S LIBERATION.
IF PEOPLE COULD READ OUR ANCIENT TEXTS, THEY WOULD REALISE THAT OUR ANCESTORS NEVER SANCTIONED CHILD MARRIAGE. THEN, THEY WOULDN'T SAY THAT OUR CULTURE DEMANDS IT.
LET'S DO THAT. LET'S PUBLISH TRANSLATIONS IN OUR JOURNAL!
THEY TRANSLATED AND PUBLISHED THE SACRED MARRIAGE TEXTS IN THREE LANGUAGES. WITH PUBLIC SUPPORT, MUTHULAKSHMI WAS ABLE TO INFLUENCE LAWS AGAINST CHILD MARRIAGE. SHE WAS ALSO RESPONSIBLE FOR INCREASING THE MINIMUM AGE FOR MARRIAGE.

ONE DAY IN JUNE, 1930, THREE YOUNG DEVADASIS TURNED UP AT HER DOORSTEP.
OUR FAMILIES ARE NOT TAKING US BACK.
WE HAVE NOWHERE TO GO. PLEASE HELP US!
MUTHULAKSHMI IMMEDIATELY TOOK THEM IN.

BUT WHEN SHE TRIED TO FIND SHELTER FOR THEM –
NO ONE IS READY TO TAKE THEM BECAUSE THEY ARE DEVADASIS. WHAT SHOULD I DO?

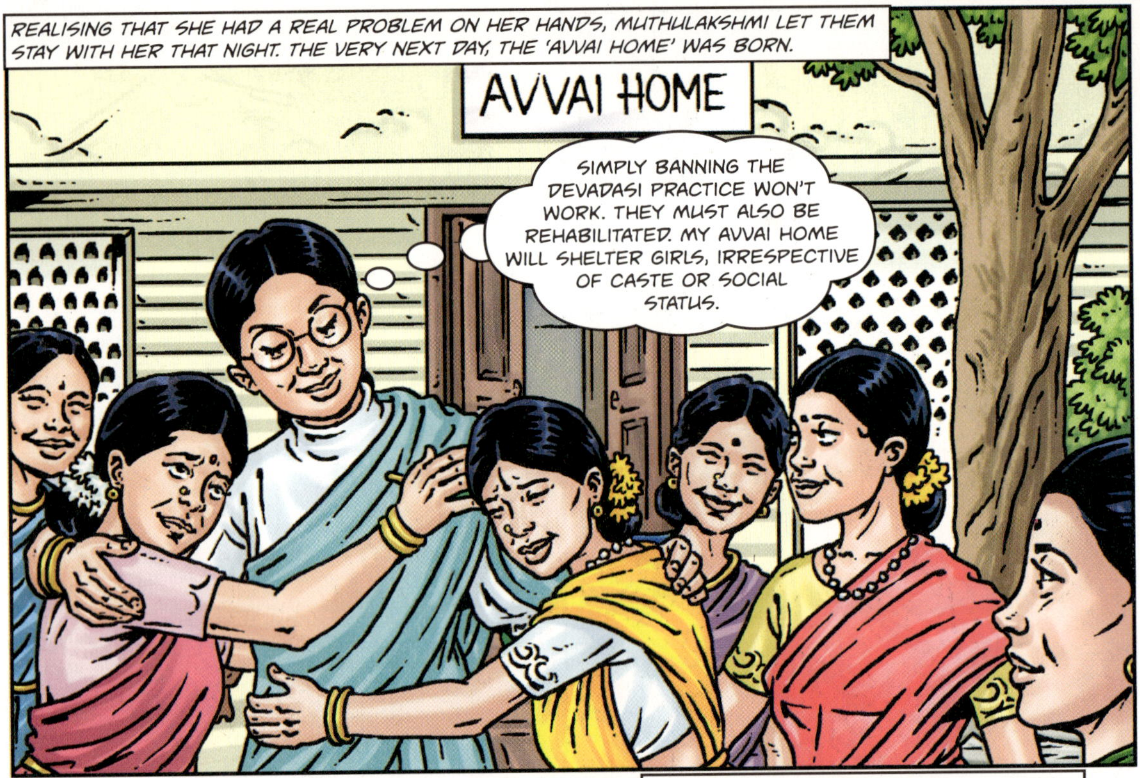

REALISING THAT SHE HAD A REAL PROBLEM ON HER HANDS, MUTHULAKSHMI LET THEM STAY WITH HER THAT NIGHT. THE VERY NEXT DAY, THE 'AVVAI HOME' WAS BORN.

AVVAI HOME

SIMPLY BANNING THE DEVADASI PRACTICE WON'T WORK. THEY MUST ALSO BE REHABILITATED. MY AVVAI HOME WILL SHELTER GIRLS, IRRESPECTIVE OF CASTE OR SOCIAL STATUS.

*ALSO KNOWN AS THE ADYAR CANCER HOSPITAL

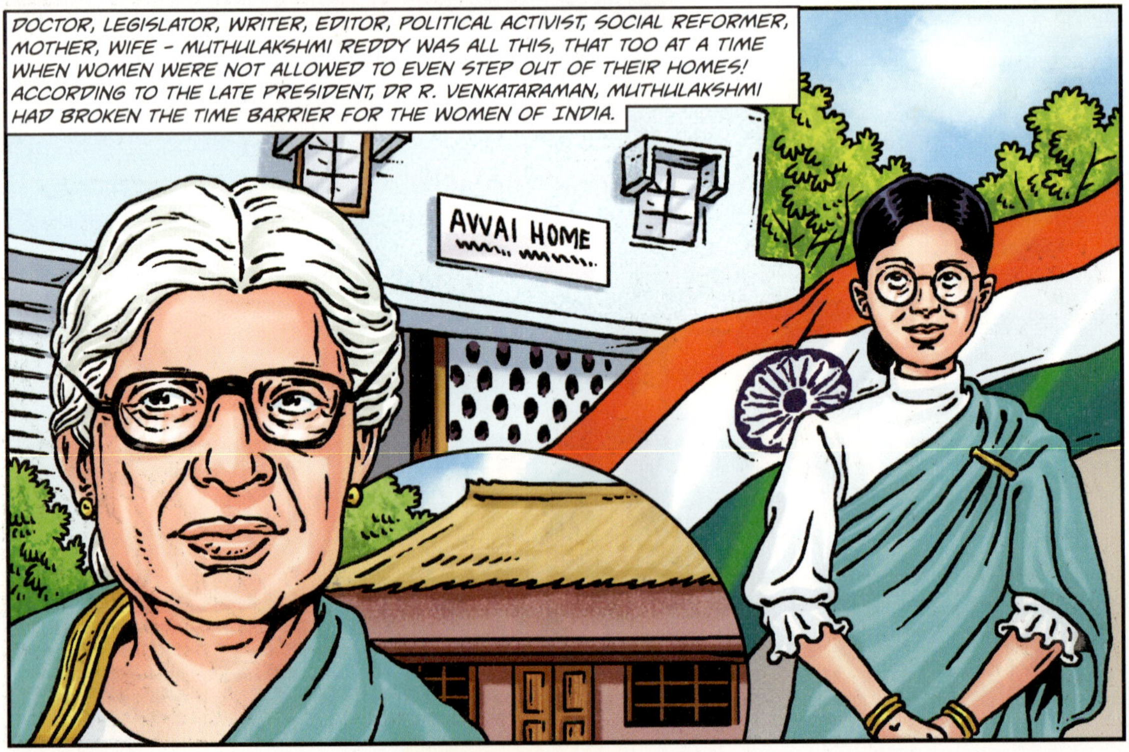

DOCTOR, LEGISLATOR, WRITER, EDITOR, POLITICAL ACTIVIST, SOCIAL REFORMER, MOTHER, WIFE – MUTHULAKSHMI REDDY WAS ALL THIS, THAT TOO AT A TIME WHEN WOMEN WERE NOT ALLOWED TO EVEN STEP OUT OF THEIR HOMES! ACCORDING TO THE LATE PRESIDENT, DR R. VENKATARAMAN, MUTHULAKSHMI HAD BROKEN THE TIME BARRIER FOR THE WOMEN OF INDIA.

AVVAI HOME

Anasuya Sarabhai - Pioneer of the labour movement in India

*GUJARATI FOR SISTER
^ELDER SISTER

*BROTHER IN GUJARATI; THIS IS HOW ANASUYA ADDRESSED HIM ALL HER LIFE.

HOW DOES IT MATTER WHAT THEY SAY? AT LEAST YOU WILL GET TO LIVE YOUR LIFE! YOU KNOW THAT FATHER AND MOTHER HAVE LEFT SOME MONEY FOR US. WE DON'T HAVE TO BE DEPENDENT ON ANYONE.
A FEW YEARS EARLIER, RUKHMABAI HAD FOUGHT TO GET HER MARRIAGE ANNULLED. ANASUYA DID THE SAME.

SOON -
AM I REALLY FREE?
YES, THE DIVORCE IS THROUGH. NOW GO BECOME THE DOCTOR YOU ALWAYS WANTED TO BE.

IN 1912, WITH HER BROTHER'S SUPPORT, ANASUYA SET SAIL FOR ENGLAND WHERE SHE WAS TO STUDY MEDICINE.
NO AMOUNT OF MONEY WOULD HAVE MADE THIS POSSIBLE IF NOT FOR THE WOMEN WHO STRUGGLED BEFORE ME.

BUT A SHOCK AWAITED HER IN ENGLAND.
IT'S CALLED DISSECTION. HOW DO YOU EXPECT TO BECOME A DOCTOR IF YOU DON'T STUDY THE BODY?
UGH! DO I HAVE TO CUT OPEN THAT DEAD ANIMAL?

*FOLLOWER OF JAINISM, A RELIGION THAT REVERES NON-VIOLENCE

*A MOVEMENT FIGHTING FOR WOMEN'S RIGHT TO VOTE

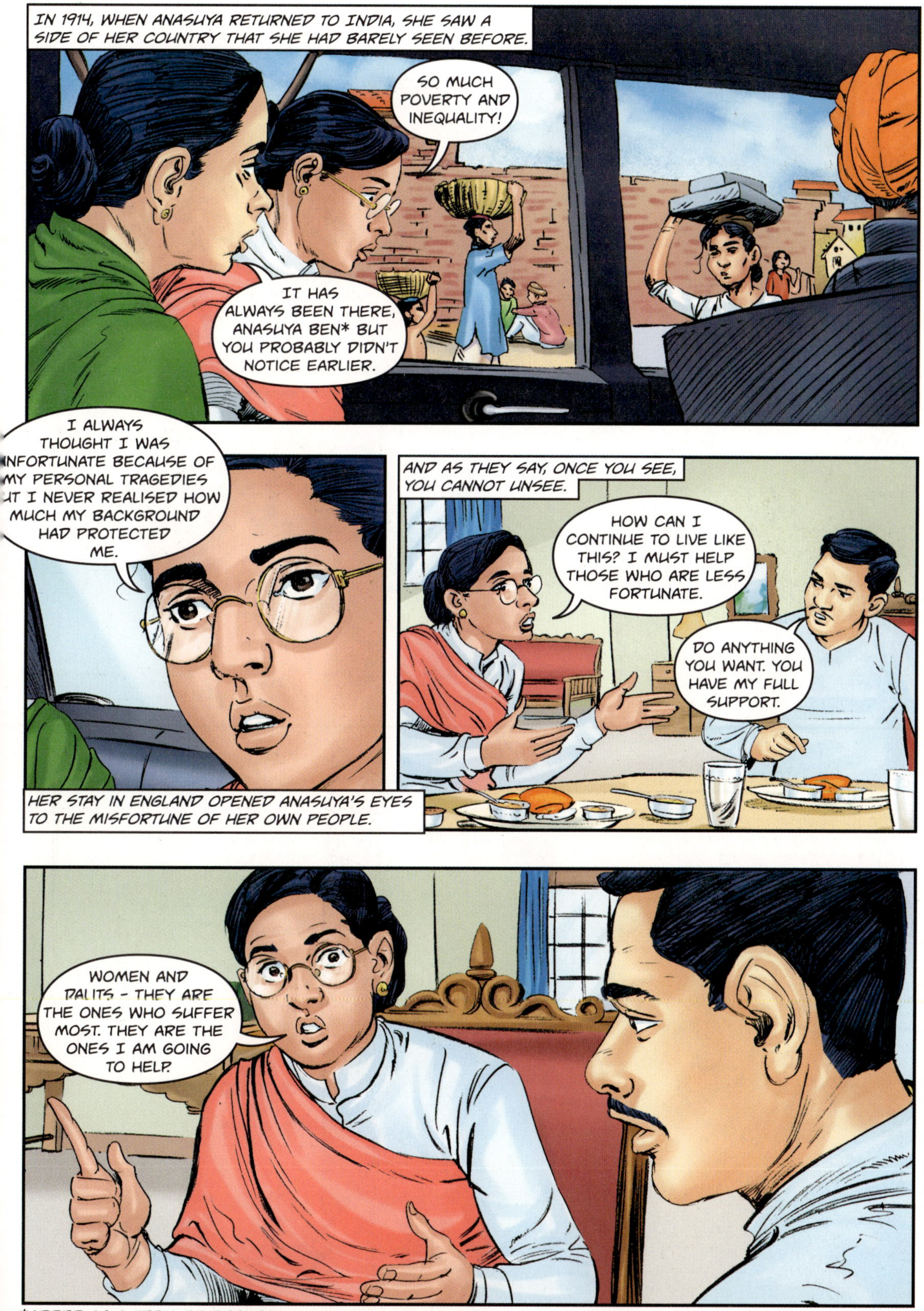

IN 1914, WHEN ANASUYA RETURNED TO INDIA, SHE SAW A SIDE OF HER COUNTRY THAT SHE HAD BARELY SEEN BEFORE.

SO MUCH POVERTY AND INEQUALITY!

IT HAS ALWAYS BEEN THERE, ANASUYA BEN* BUT YOU PROBABLY DIDN'T NOTICE EARLIER.

I ALWAYS THOUGHT I WAS UNFORTUNATE BECAUSE OF MY PERSONAL TRAGEDIES BUT I NEVER REALISED HOW MUCH MY BACKGROUND HAD PROTECTED ME.

HER STAY IN ENGLAND OPENED ANASUYA'S EYES TO THE MISFORTUNE OF HER OWN PEOPLE.

AND AS THEY SAY, ONCE YOU SEE, YOU CANNOT UNSEE.

HOW CAN I CONTINUE TO LIVE LIKE THIS? I MUST HELP THOSE WHO ARE LESS FORTUNATE.

DO ANYTHING YOU WANT. YOU HAVE MY FULL SUPPORT.

*ADDED AS A TERM OF RESPECT

SHE SET UP A SCHOOL FOR CHILDREN OF ALL CASTES. TO TEACH THEM ABOUT HYGIENE, SHE WOULD BATHE THEM HERSELF. SHE OPENED A HOSTEL FOR DALIT GIRLS AND BUILT CRECHES AND PUBLIC TOILETS FOR WOMEN.

ONE MORNING, AS SHE SAT COMBING THE HAIR OF HER SCHOOL CHILDREN –
UH!
OH!
??

ANASUYA WATCHED AS MEN AND WOMEN STUMBLED AND FELL AS THEY STRUGGLED TO WALK.
WHAT'S HAPPENING? ARE ALL OF THEM ILL?

WHY ARE YOU ALL LIKE THIS? WHERE ARE YOU COMING FROM?
FROM THE FACTORY ...UH!

BEN, BEN... ARE YOU OKAY?

WE'RE ALL EXHAUSTED. SHE'LL FEEL BETTER ONCE SHE EATS SOMETHING.
BUT WHAT HAPPENED? WHY ARE YOU ALL SO TIRED?

WE'VE BEEN WORKING FOR TWO WHOLE DAYS WITHOUT A BREAK, BEN.
WHAT?
THE WORKERS HAD BEEN WORKING FOR 36 HOURS STRAIGHT! THEY HAD NOT HAD ANY TIME OFF IN BETWEEN!

THAT IS INHUMAN. IT'S SLAVERY!

THE INCIDENT PLAYED ON ANASUYA'S MIND, UNTIL -

I CAN'T LET SUCH THINGS GO ON. I MUST DO SOMETHING!

SHE WENT TO VISIT THE MILL WORKERS AT THE SETTLEMENT WHERE THEY LIVED.

WHAT SHE SAW SHOCKED HER.

UH!

THE WORKERS WERE LIVING IN BARE, CRAMPED SPACES. THERE WAS NO CLEAN WATER OR FOOD, ONLY FILTH AND DESPAIR.

*OWNERS/BOSSES

PROTEST. DEMAND YOUR FAIR SHARE. AND IF THEY DON'T GIVE IT TO YOU, STOP GOING TO WORK.
YES, DON'T GO TO WORK. IF ALL OF YOU DON'T GO, THEY WILL HAVE TO LISTEN TO YOU.

WHAT?
!
?
ANASUYA WAS SUGGESTING THAT THE WEAVERS GO ON A STRIKE IF PROTESTING DID NOT WORK. THIS WAS A VERY UNUSUAL THOUGHT...

...BUT IT TOOK ROOT, AND SOON –
YOU HAVE TO MAKE YOUR VOICES HEARD. THE OWNERS MUST RECOGNISE YOUR IMPORTANCE. THEY MUST GIVE YOU YOUR BONUS.

GIVE US OUR BONUS!
GIVE US OUR BONUS!

IS THAT ANASUYA BEN? BUT SHE'S ONE OF US!
SHE WAS. AND YET HER SENSE OF SOCIAL JUSTICE HAD MADE HER CROSS OVER TO THE OTHER SIDE.

BUT THE MILL OWNERS DID NOT LISTEN TO HER AND SOON THE WORKERS DECIDED TO STRIKE.
IF THEY STRIKE, I WILL BE TRULY PLACED AGAINST MY BELOVED BHAI. WHAT SHOULD I DO? HE IS THE ONE WHO HAS SUPPORTED ME ALL MY LIFE...

...BUT THEY ARE THE ONES WITHOUT SUPPORT.

THAT NIGHT AT HOME -
THIS FIGHT IS NOT AGAINST YOU, BHAI. I HAVE TO DO WHAT IS RIGHT.
I KNOW.

FOR MORE THAN 20 DAYS, ANASUYA CAMPAIGNED TIRELESSLY FOR THE WEAVERS' RIGHTS. SHE WAS SET AGAINST HER OWN PEOPLE BUT HER DIGNITY AND REASONING WON HER ADMIRERS ON BOTH SIDES. FINALLY -
WE AGREE TO YOUR DEMANDS. YOU WILL ALL GET A 20 PER CENT BONUS.

THE WORKERS WERE ECSTATIC!

ANASUYA BEN, WE OWE IT ALL TO YOU.
YOU TAKE CARE OF EVERY NEED OF OURS. YOU ARE NOT ANASUYA BEN, YOU ARE OUR MOTABEN.
YES, YES! MOTABEN, OUR GUARDIAN!
FROM THAT DAY, ANASUYA CAME TO BE KNOWN AS MOTABEN OR 'ELDER SISTER', ONE WHO ALWAYS LOOKS AFTER OTHERS.

IT WAS IN THOSE YEARS THAT MOHANDAS KARAMCHAND GANDHI FOUND HIS WAY BACK TO INDIA AND TO AHMEDABAD.
I WOULD LIKE TO BUILD AN ASHRAM HERE ON THE BANKS OF THE SABARMATI.
AMONG THE FIRST TO HELP HIM WERE THE BROTHER-SISTER DUO AMBALAL AND ANASUYA. OVER TIME, THE THREE BECAME VERY CLOSE.

SO IN 1918, WHEN THE MILL OWNERS DECIDED TO STOP THE PLAGUE BONUS THEY HAD BEEN GIVING THEIR WORKERS, ANASUYA HAD GANDHIJI'S SUPPORT. BY THEN, AMBALAL HAD BECOME THE PRESIDENT OF THE MILL OWNERS ASSOCIATION.
THEY ALREADY HAVE SO LITTLE. HOW CAN YOU TAKE BACK WHAT YOU HAVE GIVEN THEM?
PRICES OF EVERYTHING HAVE GONE UP. HOW WILL THEY SURVIVE?
IF YOU TAKE AWAY THEIR BONUS, YOU MUST INCREASE THEIR SALARY.
THAT'S SIMPLY NOT POSSIBLE, ANASUYA BEN! DO YOU KNOW HOW MANY WORKERS THERE ARE? WE WILL GO BANKRUPT.
SHE'S READY TO FIGHT HER BROTHER FOR A CAUSE. THAT TAKES COURAGE. SHE IS 'PUJYA'*!
ANASUYA WAS THE ONLY WOMAN GANDHI ADDRESSED AS PUJYA. WHAT SET ANASUYA APART FROM LATER TRADE UNIONISTS WAS THAT INSTEAD OF CONFRONTATION, SHE USED THE PATH OF UNDERSTANDING AND MUTUAL RESPECT.
A FEW DAYS LATER -
THE WORKERS ARE ASKING FOR A 50 PER CENT INCREASE IN THEIR WAGES.
THAT MIGHT BE TOO MUCH BUT LET'S FIND OUT.

*REVERED

ONE WEEK LATER -
50 PER CENT IS SIMPLY NOT REASONABLE.
35 PER CENT.
YES, WE CALCULATED THEIR NEEDS ALONG WITH RISING COSTS. 35 PER CENT IS THE BARE MINIMUM THAT THEY NEED.

20 PER CENT.
WE ARE NOT HERE TO BARGAIN. THE LIVES OF THE WORKERS ARE AT STAKE.
NOTHING LESS THAN 35 PER CENT WILL DO.
FOR MORE THAN THREE WEEKS, THOUSANDS OF WORKERS SAT ON THE BANKS OF THE SABARMATI INSTEAD OF GOING TO WORK.

INITIALLY EXCITED, THEY SOON BEGAN TO LOSE THEIR MORALE.
THERE IS NO MONEY LEFT.
WE HAVEN'T EATEN IN SO LONG.
MA, MY HEAD HURTS!

IF THIS GOES ON MUCH LONGER, THE WORKERS MIGHT RESORT TO VIOLENCE.
YES, WE MUST REACH A SETTLEMENT SOON.
THIS STRIKE WAS ALSO THE FIRST TIME THAT GANDHI WAS PUTTING HIS IDEAS OF NON-VIOLENCE INTO PRACTICE.

ONE DAY -
WE DON'T HAVE ANY FOOD LEFT AND LOOK AT YOU TWO EATING SO WELL. SHAME ON YOU!
UH!

THEY ARE RIGHT. HOW CAN WE EXPECT THEM TO FIGHT WHEN WE ARE NOT REALLY WITH THEM?

FROM TODAY, I WILL ALSO GO ON A FAST. UNTIL YOU GET MONEY FOR FOOD, I WILL NOT EAT AS WELL.
THIS LED TO THE IDEA OF THE HUNGER STRIKE THAT MAHATMA GANDHI WAS TO USE SO EFFECTIVELY DURING THE FREEDOM STRUGGLE.

*ALSO KNOWN AS AHMEDABAD TEXTILE LABOUR ASSOCIATION OR TLA, IT IS GUJARAT'S OLDEST LABOUR UNION.

^ IN ANASUYA'S MEMORY, ELA BHATT HAS ESTABLISHED A PERMANENT EXHIBITION ON HER LIFE.

**SELF-EMPLOYED WOMEN'S ASSOCIATION OF INDIA

Janaki Ammal - First Indian woman botanist

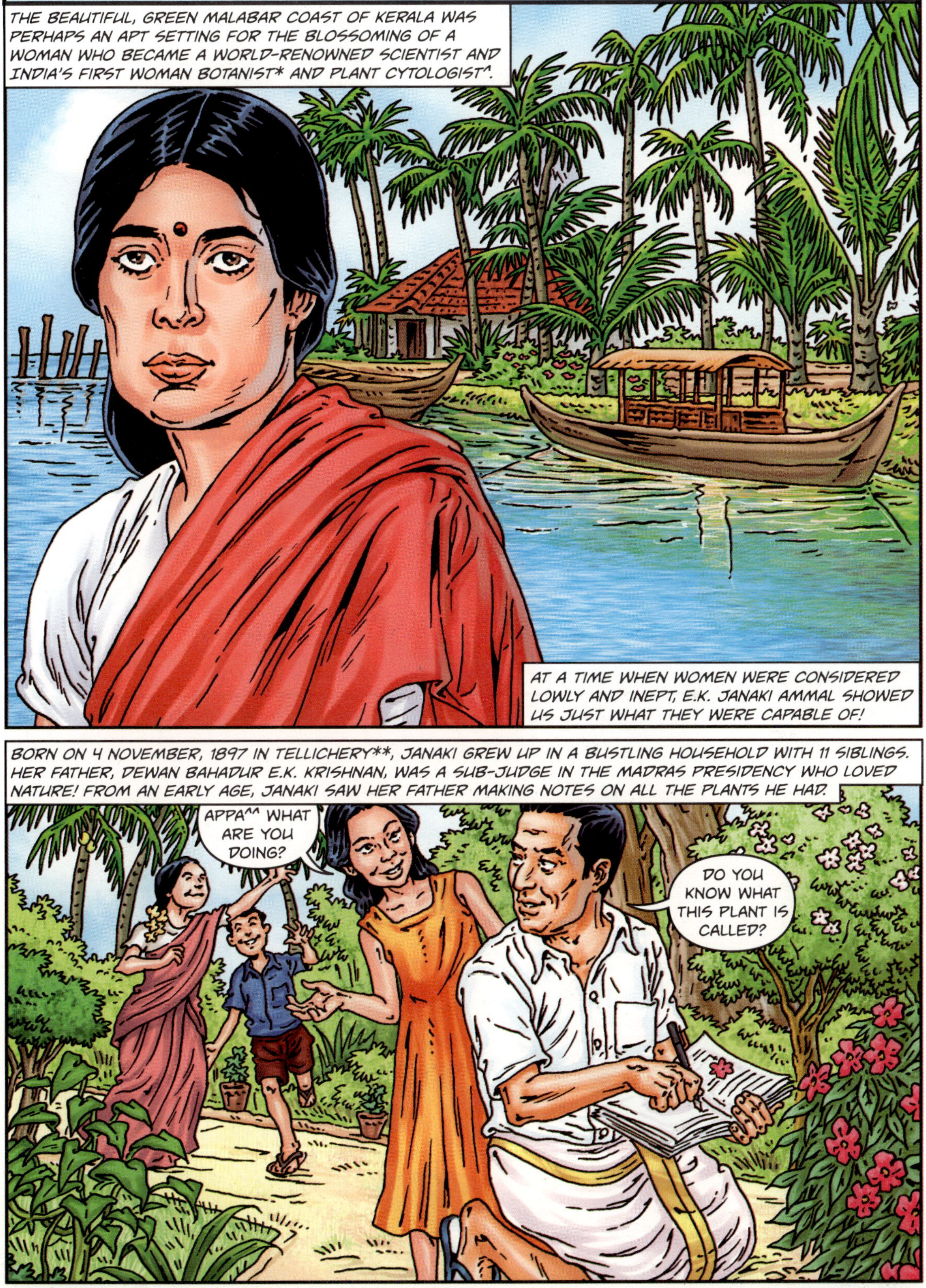

THE BEAUTIFUL, GREEN MALABAR COAST OF KERALA WAS PERHAPS AN APT SETTING FOR THE BLOSSOMING OF A WOMAN WHO BECAME A WORLD-RENOWNED SCIENTIST AND INDIA'S FIRST WOMAN BOTANIST* AND PLANT CYTOLOGIST^.

AT A TIME WHEN WOMEN WERE CONSIDERED LOWLY AND INEPT, E.K. JANAKI AMMAL SHOWED US JUST WHAT THEY WERE CAPABLE OF!

BORN ON 4 NOVEMBER, 1897 IN TELLICHERY**, JANAKI GREW UP IN A BUSTLING HOUSEHOLD WITH 11 SIBLINGS. HER FATHER, DEWAN BAHADUR E.K. KRISHNAN, WAS A SUB-JUDGE IN THE MADRAS PRESIDENCY WHO LOVED NATURE! FROM AN EARLY AGE, JANAKI SAW HER FATHER MAKING NOTES ON ALL THE PLANTS HE HAD.

*A PERSON WHO STUDIES PLANTS
^A PERSON WHO STUDIES CELLS
**NOW KNOWN AS THALASSERY
^^FATHER IN MALAYALAM

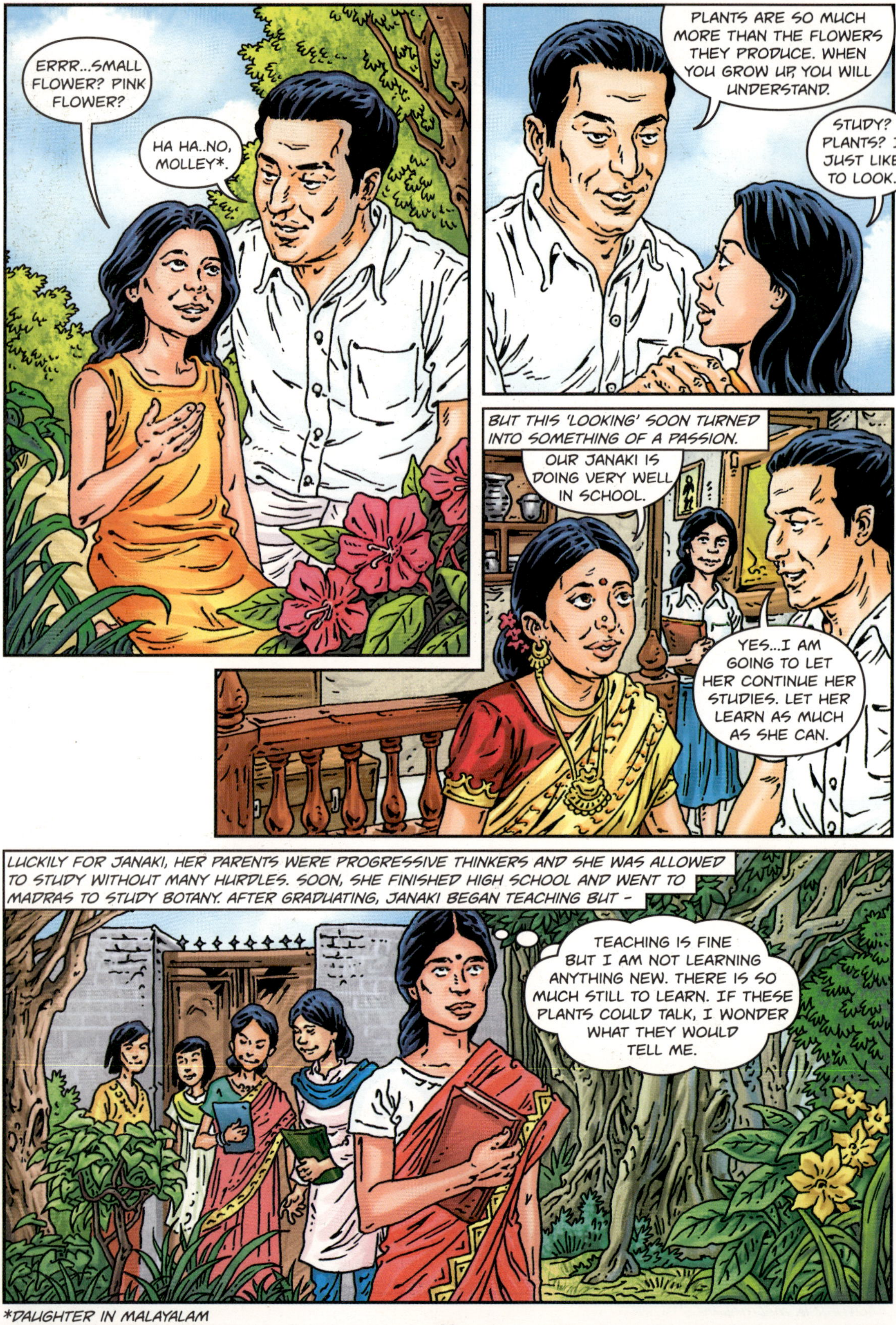

ERRR...SMALL FLOWER? PINK FLOWER?

HA HA..NO, MOLLEY*.

PLANTS ARE SO MUCH MORE THAN THE FLOWERS THEY PRODUCE. WHEN YOU GROW UP, YOU WILL UNDERSTAND.

STUDY? PLANTS? I JUST LIKE TO LOOK.

BUT THIS 'LOOKING' SOON TURNED INTO SOMETHING OF A PASSION.

OUR JANAKI IS DOING VERY WELL IN SCHOOL.

YES...I AM GOING TO LET HER CONTINUE HER STUDIES. LET HER LEARN AS MUCH AS SHE CAN.

LUCKILY FOR JANAKI, HER PARENTS WERE PROGRESSIVE THINKERS AND SHE WAS ALLOWED TO STUDY WITHOUT MANY HURDLES. SOON, SHE FINISHED HIGH SCHOOL AND WENT TO MADRAS TO STUDY BOTANY. AFTER GRADUATING, JANAKI BEGAN TEACHING BUT -

*DAUGHTER IN MALAYALAM

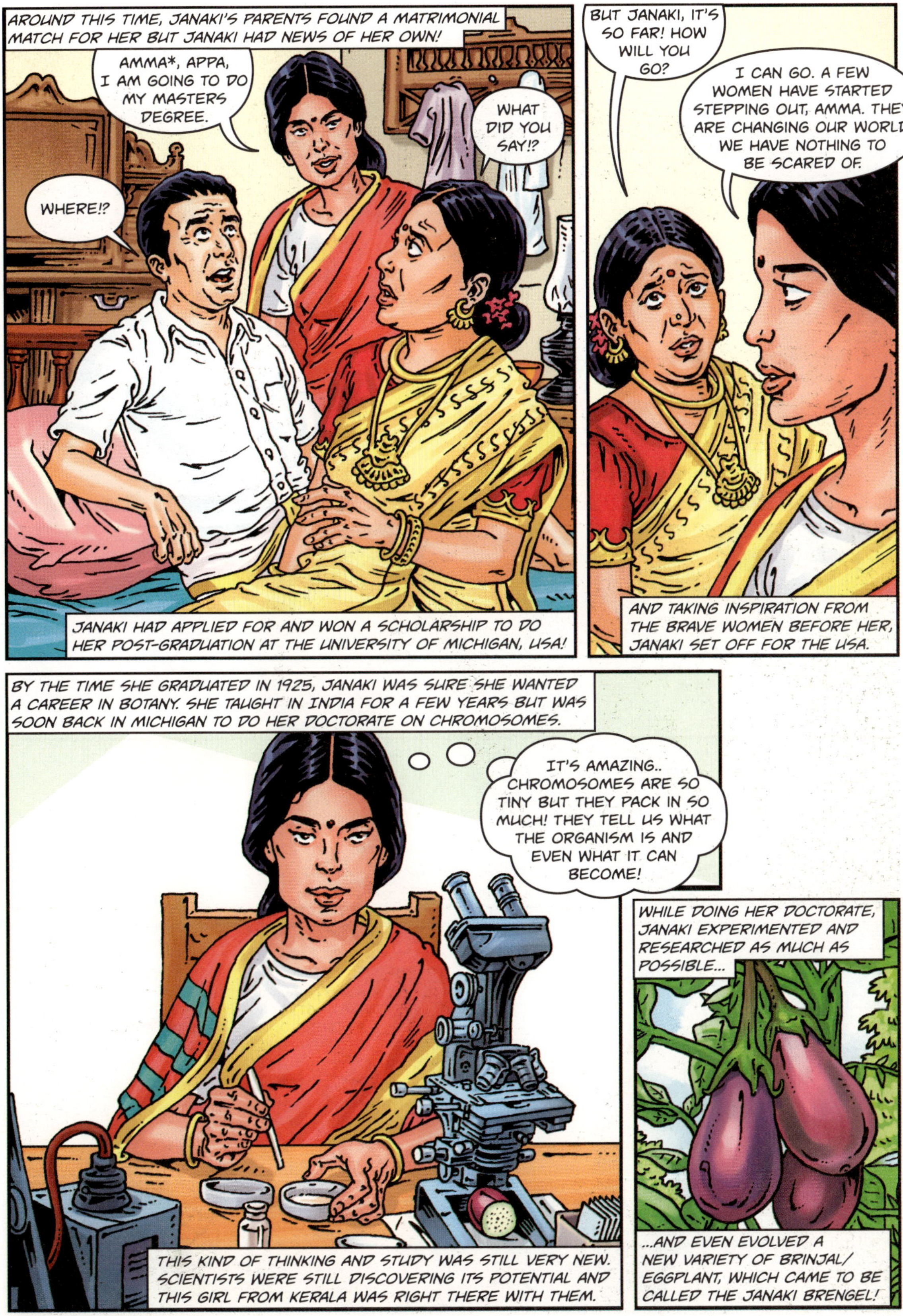

BY THE TIME SHE GRADUATED IN 1925, JANAKI WAS SURE SHE WANTED A CAREER IN BOTANY. SHE TAUGHT IN INDIA FOR A FEW YEARS BUT WAS SOON BACK IN MICHIGAN TO DO HER DOCTORATE ON CHROMOSOMES.

IT'S AMAZING.. CHROMOSOMES ARE SO TINY BUT THEY PACK IN SO MUCH! THEY TELL US WHAT THE ORGANISM IS AND EVEN WHAT IT CAN BECOME!

THIS KIND OF THINKING AND STUDY WAS STILL VERY NEW. SCIENTISTS WERE STILL DISCOVERING ITS POTENTIAL AND THIS GIRL FROM KERALA WAS RIGHT THERE WITH THEM.

WHILE DOING HER DOCTORATE, JANAKI EXPERIMENTED AND RESEARCHED AS MUCH AS POSSIBLE...

...AND EVEN EVOLVED A NEW VARIETY OF BRINJAL/ EGGPLANT, WHICH CAME TO BE CALLED THE JANAKI BRENGEL!

*MOTHER IN MALAYALAM

*DOCTOR OF SCIENCE

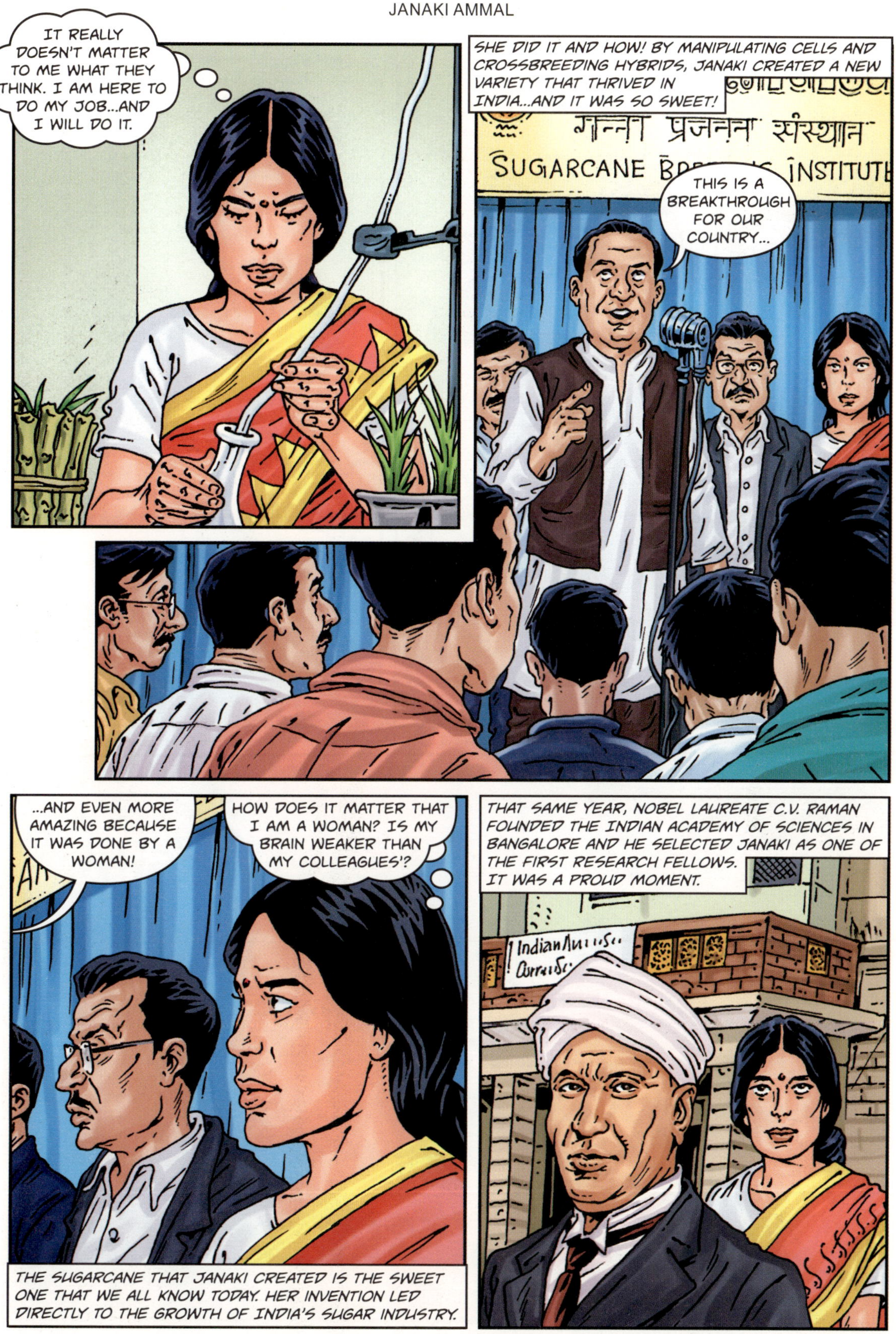

IT REALLY DOESN'T MATTER TO ME WHAT THEY THINK. I AM HERE TO DO MY JOB...AND I WILL DO IT.

SHE DID IT AND HOW! BY MANIPULATING CELLS AND CROSSBREEDING HYBRIDS, JANAKI CREATED A NEW VARIETY THAT THRIVED IN INDIA...AND IT WAS SO SWEET!

गन्ना प्रजनन संस्थान

THIS IS A BREAKTHROUGH FOR OUR COUNTRY...

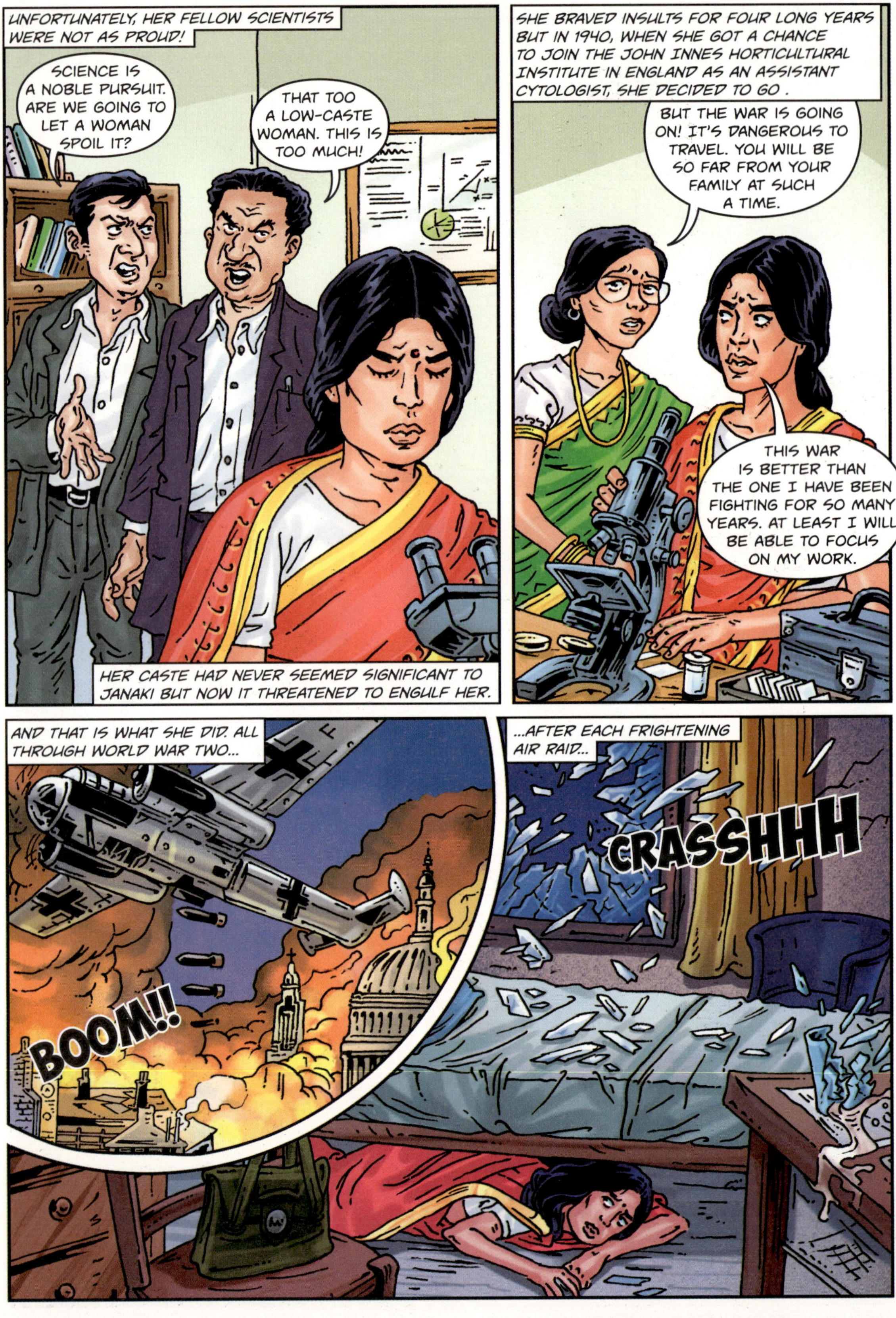

SHE BRAVED INSULTS FOR FOUR LONG YEARS BUT IN 1940, WHEN SHE GOT A CHANCE TO JOIN THE JOHN INNES HORTICULTURAL INSTITUTE IN ENGLAND AS AN ASSISTANT CYTOLOGIST, SHE DECIDED TO GO .

BUT THE WAR IS GOING ON! IT'S DANGEROUS TO TRAVEL. YOU WILL BE SO FAR FROM YOUR FAMILY AT SUCH A TIME.

THIS WAR IS BETTER THAN THE ONE I HAVE BEEN FIGHTING FOR SO MANY YEARS. AT LEAST I WILL BE ABLE TO FOCUS ON MY WORK.

AND THAT IS WHAT SHE DID. ALL THROUGH WORLD WAR TWO...

BOOM!!

...AFTER EACH FRIGHTENING AIR RAID...

CRASSHHH

*KEW GARDENS IS A TREASURE HOUSE OF PLANT SPECIMENS FROM AROUND THE WORLD.

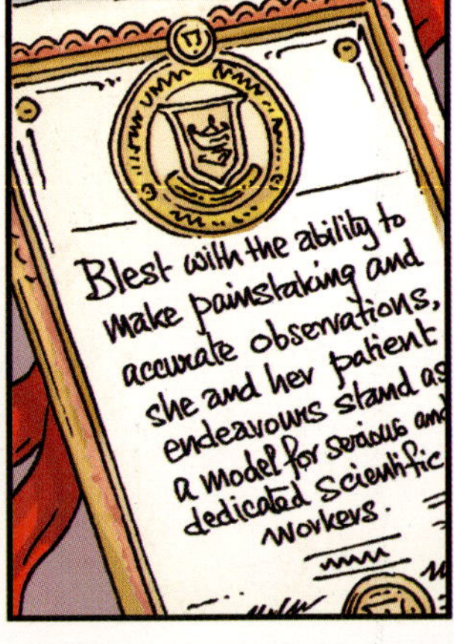

*DOCTOR OF LAWS

THROUGH IT ALL, JANAKI REMAINED HUMBLE AND DEDICATED TO HER WORK. SHE STILL PLACED HER LOVE FOR NATURE ABOVE EVERYTHING ELSE.
JANAKI, YOU ARE PROTESTING AGAINST THE SILENT VALLEY DAM? THAT WILL NOT MAKE THE GOVERNMENT HAPPY.
EVERYTHING I AM IS BECAUSE OF THE ENVIRONMENT, NOT BECAUSE OF THE GOVERNMENT.
THE GOVERNMENT WAS BUILDING A DAM IN KERALA'S SILENT VALLEY...AND JANAKI, AWARE OF THE DANGERS TO THE ECOSYSTEM, WAS ONE OF THE MAIN PROTESTORS.
DESPITE HER PROTEST, SHE WAS AWARDED THE PADMA SHRI IN 1977. BY THEN SHE HAD RETIRED, BUT CONTINUED TO WORK AS SCIENTIST EMERITUS AT MADRAS UNIVERSITY UNTIL HER DEATH IN FEBRUARY, 1984.
IN MEMORIAM, THE NATIONAL AWARD IN TAXONOMY IS GIVEN EVERY YEAR IN HER NAME. A HERBARIUM IN JAMMU WITH OVER 25,000 SPECIES HAS BEEN DEDICATED TO HER. EVERY YEAR, THE JOHN INNES CENTRE IN ENGLAND AWARDS THE JANAKIAMMAL SCHOLARSHIPS TO POST-GRADUATE RESEARCH STUDENTS FROM DEVELOPING COUNTRIES.
SIMPLE, HUMBLE, AND BRILLIANT, HER WHOLE LIFE WAS DEVOTED TO THE STUDY OF PLANTS. BEING A WOMAN WAS A HANDICAP AT THE TIME THAT JANAKI LIVED. VIEWED AS WEAK AND INCAPABLE OF SCIENTIFIC STUDY, WOMEN STAYED IN THE SHADOWS. JANAKI NOT ONLY SHOWED THAT SHE WAS CAPABLE BUT SHE ALSO STOOD TALL AMONG ALL THE GREATS IN HER CHOSEN FIELD AND MADE LASTING CONTRIBUTIONS THAT BENEFITTED THE WHOLE WORLD!

Anna Chandy

First woman Judge

Anna Chandy was lucky in two aspects. Born in 1905 to a Syrian Christian family in Trivandrum, Kerala, she was encouraged to study.

The second time luck knocked at her door was in the 1920s. The queen of Travancore, Maharani Sethu Lakshmi Bayi, decided to open the doors of the Government Law College to women. People were horrified, more so when young Anna decided to take up law. In 1926, she earned a postgraduate degree with distinction, becoming the first Indian female lawyer.

She chose to become a criminal lawyer, stepping firmly into a territory unfriendly to women. With her natural leaning towards justice and an ability to see the wrong in society, Anna was a success as a lawyer. Soon, she started using her voice to speak up about the injustices heaped upon women. She founded a magazine called 'Shrimati' in 1930, the first such magazine in Kerala for voices like hers. Among other issues, Anna strongly protested against the wage gap that existed between the men and women working on farms.

She soon realised that along with a voice, she also needed the power to correct those problems. With this in mind, she contested the elections from the Shree Mulam Popular Assembly in Travancore. She lost but that only strengthened her resolve. Two years later, she ran for the post again and this time, she won! Serving from 1932–1934, Anna lifted the ban on women holding government jobs.

She became the first female judge of the country in 1937, when she was appointed as a Munsif in the Travancore court. "I knew I was a test case," she said later, "If I faltered or failed, I would not just be damaging my own career but would be doing a great disservice to the cause of women."

Her hard work paid off and Anna went on to become a judge in the Kerala High Court in 1959. She was the first woman High Court judge in the entire Commonwealth! After retiring in 1967, she served in the Law Commission of India.

Anna died in 1996 at the age of 91. Articulate and fearless, Anna fought hard to ensure that Indian women have a right to choose how they live.

Kamala Sohonie

First woman doctorate

Kamala Sohonie grew up unlike other girls of her time. She was born, in 1912, into a family of distinguished scientists and was encouraged to study. In 1933, she topped Bombay University when she completed her B.Sc in chemistry and physics, after which she applied to the Indian Institute of Science (IISc) for a research fellowship. That was where the harsh reality of her gender came like a slap in the face. Nobel Laureate Prof. C.V. Raman, the Director of IISc, refused her application simply because she was a woman!

But if Prof. Raman was firm about not giving her admission, Kamala was equally firm about getting it. For days, she sat outside his office until he agreed to admit her. But he had conditions. "You will be on probation for one year, you will work only at night so as not to disrupt the atmosphere of the campus, and finally, you must conduct yourself 'honourably'," he said. Humiliated but with no choice, Kamala had to agree. She passed her M.Sc with distinction. Very soon, the gates of IISc and other science institutes were opened to women. A quiet revolution had taken place.

Kamala went on to study at Cambridge University where her discovery of cytochrome C, which helps plants in respiration, helped her get a doctorate. She was the first Indian woman to be awarded a Ph.D.

Kamala then came back to take part in the Indian freedom struggle. After she got married in 1947, she joined the Royal Institute of Science in Bombay. All along, she had been working on finding a way to improve the diet of the poor. On a request from the then President of India, Dr Rajendra Prasad, she started studying the nutritional benefits of 'neera' (sap from the palm tree) and discovered that it had significant amounts of iron and vitamins A and C. She found a way to include this in the diet of malnourished people. For this discovery, Kamala won the President's Award.

She made history when she became the Director of the Institute of Science in Bombay – the first lady to head such a premier scientific institution.

In 1998, at a ceremony organised to felicitate her, Kamala collapsed. She passed away a few days later. Thus came to an end a life that quietly challenged society's norms and steadily worked to enrich the life of India's masses.

Anna Mani - First woman meteorologist

SHE WAS ONLY SEVEN WHEN -
I HAVE NOTHING TO DO!
WHY? WHERE ARE YOUR BOOKS?

I HAVE FINISHED READING THEM.
THERE ARE MANY MORE IN THE TOWN LIBRARY.

THOSE ARE THE ONES I HAVE FINISHED!
SEE APPA, YOUR DAUGHTER HAS READ ALL THE BOOKS IN THE TOWN LIBRARY.
ANNA HAD FINISHED READING ALL THE BOOKS IN HER MOTHER TONGUE, MALAYALAM. THIS WAS THE ONLY LANGUAGE SHE KNEW UNTIL THEN.

IS THAT SO? YOU WILL HAVE TO LEARN ANOTHER LANGUAGE THEN.
I WILL LEARN ENGLISH! THERE ARE MANY BOOKS IN ENGLISH.
SO ANNA STARTED LEARNING ENGLISH, JUST SO THAT SHE COULD READ MORE.

*THE VAIKOM SATYAGRAHA WAS A RESISTANCE PUT UP BY THE PEOPLE OF TRAVANCORE TO PROTEST AGAINST THE BRAHMINS WHO HAD BANNED DALITS FROM WALKING ON THE ROAD OUTSIDE THEIR TEMPLE.

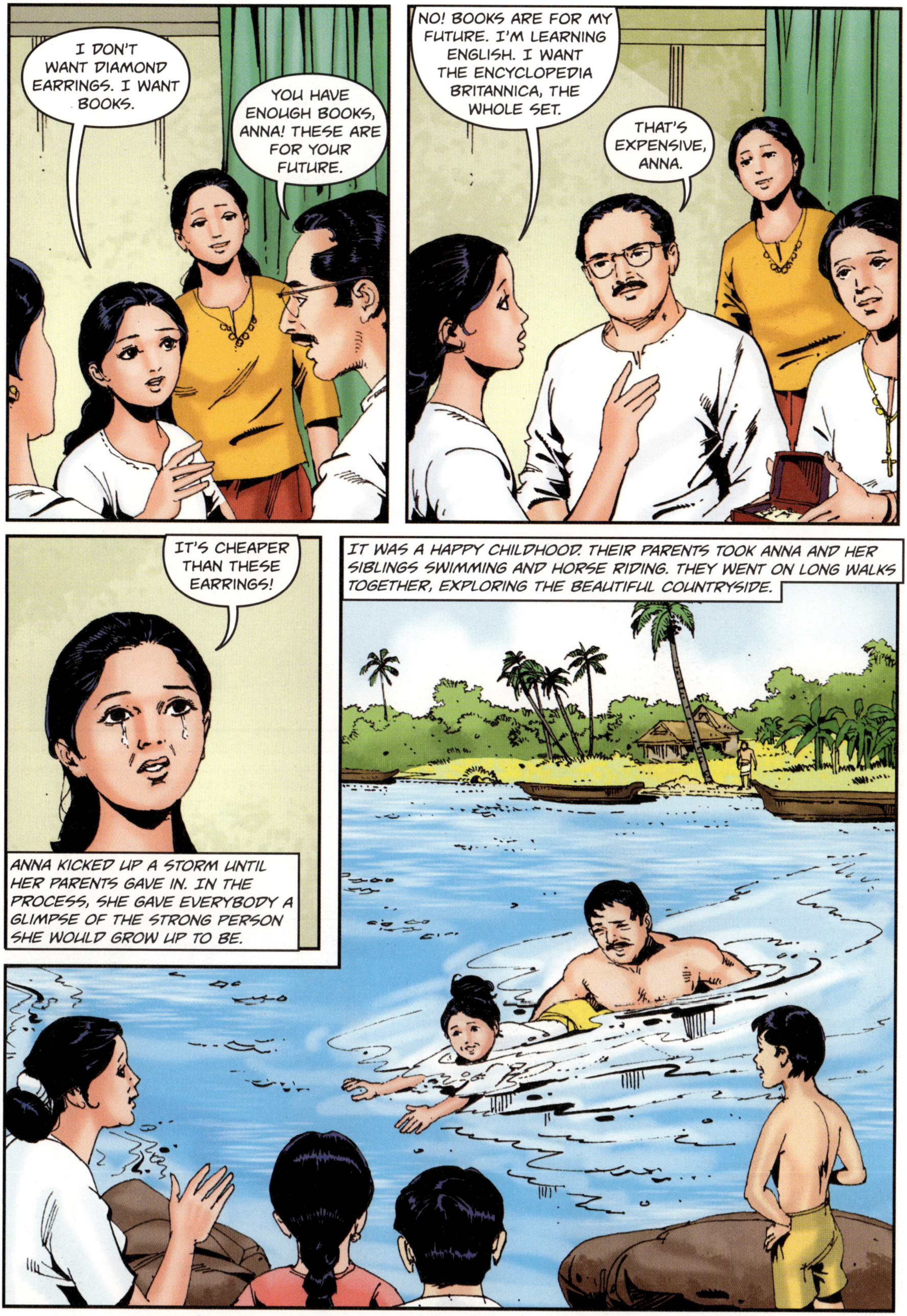

IT'S CHEAPER THAN THESE EARRINGS!

ANNA KICKED UP A STORM UNTIL HER PARENTS GAVE IN. IN THE PROCESS, SHE GAVE EVERYBODY A GLIMPSE OF THE STRONG PERSON SHE WOULD GROW UP TO BE.

IT WAS A HAPPY CHILDHOOD. THEIR PARENTS TOOK ANNA AND HER SIBLINGS SWIMMING AND HORSE RIDING. THEY WENT ON LONG WALKS TOGETHER, EXPLORING THE BEAUTIFUL COUNTRYSIDE.

*HE WAS THE FIRST ASIAN TO WIN THE NOBEL PRIZE FOR PHYSICS IN 1930.

C.V. RAMAN WAS AT THAT TIME STUDYING THE SPECTROSCOPY OF DIAMONDS AND RUBIES. ANNA BECAME AN IMPORTANT PART OF THAT RESEARCH BUT THE EXPERIMENTS WERE LONG AND TEDIOUS.
HOW MANY HOURS BEFORE THE RESULTS START SHOWING?
15 AT LEAST, SUNANDA, BUT WE WILL HAVE TO KEEP MONITORING THE PROGRESS.
THERE WERE ONLY TWO OTHER WOMEN IN THE INSTITUTE AT THAT TIME. THAT WAS STILL THREE MORE THAN MOST OTHER SCIENTIFIC ESTABLISHMENTS!

YAWN...I'M GOING TO SLEEP FOR A WHILE, THEN YOU CAN SLEEP AND I'LL DO THE MONITORING.
OKAY.

SUNANDA CURLED UP TO SLEEP BUT UNDER THE DESK WHERE THE EXPERIMENTS WERE BEING CONDUCTED -

THIS IS SO SAD. I WISH WE WERE ALLOWED TO GO OUT INTO THE LAWNS TO REST.
THIS WAS THE PRICE THAT THE ENTERPRISING WOMEN HAD TO PAY. THEY WERE BEING ALLOWED TO STUDY AND WORK BUT WERE NOT ALLOWED TO RELAX OUTSIDE THEIR LABS, LEST THEY INTERACT WITH MALE SCIENTISTS!

BUT PROGRESS HAPPENS IN SMALL STEPS AND ANNA WAS HAPPY THAT SHE WAS AT LEAST BEING ALLOWED TO DO SOMETHING PRODUCTIVE WITH HER LIFE. SHE WORKED HARD AND THREE YEARS LATER –
YOUR THESIS? IT'S READY?
YES, SIR.

IN THE THREE YEARS (1942–45) THAT ANNA WAS THERE, SHE AUTHORED FIVE RESEARCH PAPERS AND COMPLETED HER PH.D THESIS. SOME DAYS LATER –
I'M SORRY BUT THE GOVERNMENT IS NOT GRANTING YOU A PH.D.
HUH? WHY?

THEY SAY YOU HAVE NOT COMPLETED YOUR POST-GRADUATION, WHICH IS TRUE.
BUT WORKING AT THIS INSTITUTE IS LIKE A POST-GRADUATION. OTHERS HAVE GOT THEIR PH.D.

I'M REALLY SORRY. THERE IS NOTHING I CAN DO.
NOTHING WAS SAID DIRECTLY BUT MANY BELIEVE THAT THE ONLY REASON SHE DID NOT GET HER PH.D WAS BECAUSE SHE WAS A WOMAN.

ANNA WAS SHOCKED BUT SHE WAS ALSO PRACTICAL.
NEVER MIND, SUNANDA. ONE PIECE OF PAPER WON'T MAKE A DIFFERENCE TO MY LIFE. WHAT I LEARNT HERE WILL ALWAYS HELP ME.

REFUSING TO LET THE SETBACK BRING HER DOWN, ANNA APPLIED FOR A SCHOLARSHIP TO STUDY PHYSICS IN ENGLAND. SHE GOT A SCHOLARSHIP BUT JUST BEFORE SHE WAS TO LEAVE –
THERE'S BEEN A MISTAKE. THERE IS NO SCHOLARSHIP AVAILABLE FOR PHYSICS.
WHAT? WHY?

AM I BEING REJECTED AGAIN SIMPLY BECAUSE I AM A WOMAN?

THERE IS ONLY ONE SCHOLARSHIP AVAILABLE BUT IT'S FOR METEOROLOGY.
METEOROLOGY!?

IN THE THICK OF THE FREEDOM STRUGGLE, ANNA MADE HER WAY TO ENGLAND ABOARD A TROOP SHIP. FOR TWO YEARS, SHE STUDIED THE SCIENCE OF METEOROLOGY, WHICH MADE HER VERY AWARE OF THE IMPACT OF WEATHER ON HUMAN LIFE.

HER BOSS SHARED HER THOUGHTS AND SOON, ANNA WAS PUT IN CHARGE OF BUILDING PRECISION INSTRUMENTS IN INDIA.
I HAVE WORKED WITH THEM AND SEEN THEM MADE BUT I HAVE NEVER MADE ANY MYSELF. WILL I BE ABLE TO DO IT? THE THING I LACK IS EXPERIENCE...

...BUT THAT I WILL ONLY GAIN BY GOING AHEAD AND DOING IT!
SO WITH HER PRACTICAL APPROACH TO LIFE, SHE SET ABOUT BUILDING PRECISION BAROMETERS, HYDROGRAPHS, ANEMOMETERS AND MANY OTHER INSTRUMENTS.

IN A SHORT WHILE, SHE WAS HEADING A TEAM OF MORE THAN 120 SCIENTISTS, ALL OF THEM MALE. CHEERFUL, FRIENDLY AND FIRM, SHE WAS A GOOD TEAM LEADER.
WRONG MEASUREMENTS ARE WORSE THAN NO MEASUREMENTS. IF SOMETHING CANNOT BE DONE, WE JUST HAVE TO FIND A BETTER WAY OF DOING IT.
SOON, ANNA HAD STANDARDISED THE DRAWINGS FOR MORE THAN A HUNDRED DIFFERENT INSTRUMENTS! NOT ONLY DID ANNA AND HER TEAM MAKE INDIA SELF-SUFFICIENT IN MEASURING AND COLLECTING DATA ON THE WEATHER...

...BUT SHE ALSO MADE HER MARK IN THE STUDY OF RADIATION AND OZONE. SHE WAS PART OF THE TEAM THAT DEVELOPED AN INDIAN OZONESONDE THAT ACCURATELY MEASURED THE LEVELS OF OZONE IN THE ATMOSPHERE.
AS A RESULT, BY THE TIME THE REST OF THE WORLD WOKE UP TO THE DANGERS OF THE DEPLETING OZONE LAYER, INDIA HAD ALREADY COLLECTED IMPORTANT DATA ON THE SUBJECT!

THE IMD HAD SOON BECOME ANNA'S SECOND HOME. SHE BECAME POPULAR FOR HER BRILLIANCE AND HER SENSE OF HUMOUR. IN A COMPLETELY MALE-DOMINATED FIELD, ANNA WAS TAKING MAJOR STRIDES TO THE TOP. IN EARLY 1963, SHE HAD A SURPRISE VISITOR.

WE ARE SETTING UP AN EQUATORIAL ROCKET LAUNCHING SITE AT THUMBA BUT WE CAN'T LAUNCH ROCKETS WITHOUT YOUR HELP.

IT WAS VIKRAM SARABHAI, WHO WOULD COME TO BE KNOWN AS 'THE FATHER OF THE INDIAN SPACE PROGRAM'. INDIA WAS PREPARING TO LAUNCH ITS FIRST ROCKET AND A METEOROLOGICAL OBSERVATORY WAS CRUCIAL TO ITS SUCCESS.

...AND WAS RIGHT THERE IN NOVEMBER, 1963, WHEN INDIA SUCCESSFULLY SENT ITS FIRST-EVER ROCKET INTO SPACE!

*WHEN WE BURN COAL, OIL, AND NATURAL GAS FOR ELECTRICITY OR FOR OUR CARS, WE PUT TOO MUCH HARMFUL CARBON DIOXIDE INTO THE ATMOSPHERE. THIS, AMONG OTHER THINGS, IS RESPONSIBLE FOR GLOBAL WARMING.

THE WIND AND THE SUN - ANNA STUDIED THEM BOTH. SHE IDENTIFIED LOCATIONS, SET UP EQUIPMENT AND MEASURED WIND SPEEDS IN MORE THAN 700 PLACES IN INDIA! THIS DIRECTLY HELPED INDIA HARNESS ENERGY FROM WIND...
...AND MADE INDIA THE FOURTH LARGEST PRODUCER OF WIND POWER IN THE WORLD.

FOR ALMOST 30 YEARS, ANNA WORKED AT THE IMD AND BY THE TIME SHE RETIRED IN 1976, SHE HAD BECOME THE INSTITUTE'S DEPUTY DIRECTOR. THE WORLD METEOROLOGICAL ORGANISATION AND THE INTERNATIONAL OZONE COMMISSION WOULD INVITE HER TO SHARE HER RESEARCH AND EVEN LEAD SOME OF THEIR TEAMS.

THOUGH TECHNICALLY 'RETIRED', ANNA WAS NOW BUSIER THAN EVER! SHE PUBLISHED TWO BOOKS IN THE NEXT FIVE YEARS...
Solar Radiation Over India
Anna Mani
S. Rangarajan
HANDBOOK OF SOLAR RADIATION
...WHICH WENT ON TO BECOME IMPORTANT REFERENCE BOOKS FOR STUDENTS AND SCIENTISTS IN HER FIELD.

ANNA ALSO STARTED HER OWN FACTORY TO MANUFACTURE INSTRUMENTS MEASURING WIND SPEED AND SOLAR ENERGY. SHE WAS STILL TRYING TO HELP INDIA HARNESS ALTERNATIVE RESOURCES OF ENERGY.
HER PIONEERING 30-YEAR WORK ON OZONE-LEVEL MEASUREMENTS FETCHED HER A CITATION FROM THE INTERNATIONAL OZONE COMMISSION. IN 1987, THE INDIAN NATIONAL SCIENCE ACADEMY ALSO HONOURED HER WITH THE K.R. RAMANATHAN MEMORIAL MEDAL.

ANNA DEDICATED MORE THAN 50 YEARS TO THE SCIENCE OF METEOROLOGY. IN AN INTERVIEW WITH SCIENCE HISTORIAN ABHA SUR –
WHAT IS THIS HOOPLA ABOUT WOMEN AND SCIENCE? MY BEING A WOMAN HAD ABSOLUTELY NO BEARING ON WHAT I CHOSE TO DO WITH MY LIFE.
"YOU CAN BUT DO YOUR BEST" WAS HER MOTTO THROUGHOUT HER LIFE AND SHE LIVED UP TO IT, FORCING PEOPLE TO REALISE THAT BEING A WOMAN DID NOT MEAN THAT SHE WAS HANDICAPPED IN ANY WAY.

ANNA CONTINUED TO BE ACTIVE AND WORK UNTIL THAT FATEFUL DAY IN 1996 WHEN SHE SUDDENLY SUFFERED A STROKE. SHE NEVER RECOVERED FROM IT AND ON 16 AUGUST, 2001, SHE PASSED AWAY IN THIRUVANANTHAPURAM. SHE WAS 78 YEARS OLD.

BRUSHING ASIDE ALL THE ODDS WITH GOOD HUMOUR, ANNA WORKED NOT ONLY FOR THE BENEFIT OF INDIA BUT ALSO THE WORLD. ACCORDING TO OLIVER ASHFORD OF THE WORLD METEOROLOGICAL ORGANISATION, "SHE HAD SUCH EXPERTISE OVER A WIDE RANGE OF MEASURING DEVICES. IF ONLY WE ALSO HAD AN ANNAMANIOMETER! "

A. Lalitha

First woman engineer

In 1937, a man died, leaving behind his eighteen-year-old widow and four-month-old daughter. According to the norms of the time, this should have been the last we ever heard of them. But **A. Lalitha** was stronger than her circumstances.

A child bride at 15, a single mother and widow at 18, she promised herself that her daughter would never feel the lack of a father. Picking up the broken pieces of her life, she realised that the first thing she needed was to be self-sufficient.

Her father was already a professor in the College of Engineering, Guindy. With his help, she managed to get admission there. Many eyebrows were raised and her father was forced to get approval from the British government.

But life as the sole woman in a completely male-dominated campus was lonely and challenging. So her father went one step further – he advertised in 'The Hindu' inviting other women to join the college!

In 1943, Lalitha made history by becoming the first-ever woman engineer in the country. But this was only the start of her journey.

Lalitha first joined the Central Standards Organisation of India in Shimla where one of her brothers lived. In 1948, she went to Calcutta and joined the Associate Electrical Industries.

It was in Calcutta that Lalitha got a chance to design transmission lines and work on the Bhakra Nangal Dam. In 1964, she was invited to the First International Conference of Women Engineers and Scientists (ICWES) in New York. She was the only Indian at this conference. She took it upon herself to actively encourage other Indian women engineers. When the Second International Conference was held in 1967, she managed to send five of them!

Lalitha passed away when she was just 60 years old. She inspired Indian women to study further, to carve out careers in STEM* and make themselves self-sufficient.

**Science, Technology, Engineering and Mathematics*

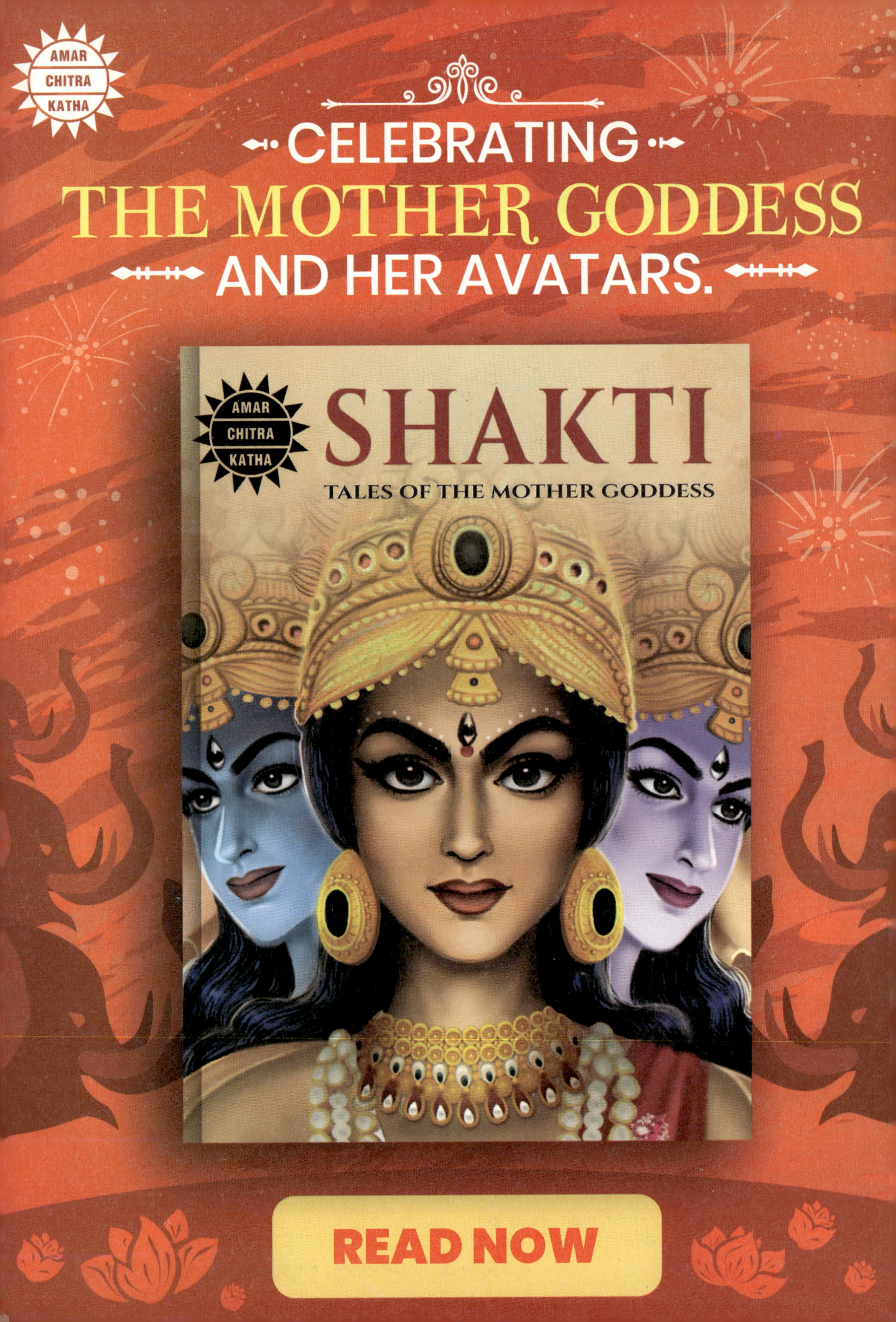